Entitled to Love

The sexual and emotional needs of the handicapped

Entitled to Love

The sexual and emotional needs of the handicapped

Wendy Greengross

NATIONAL MARRIAGE GUIDANCE COUNCIL
in association with
NATIONAL FUND FOR RESEARCH INTO
CRIPPLING DISEASES

First published 1976

First published 1976
by Malaby Press Limited
Aldine House, 26 Albemarle Street, London
© Wendy Greengross 1976
Reprinted 1976
by National Marriage Guidance Council

This book is set in IBM 11pt Journal Roman Medium

Printed in Great Britain by
Biddles Ltd, Guildford, Surrey

ISBN 0 85351 047 4

Contents

1

Introduction:
What is the problem?

Today we are living in an almost totally sex-oriented world, where the whole and beautiful are worshipped and admired, and where idyllic personal relationships and ecstatic sexual satisfaction are glorified as the modern symbols of success. A certain washing-up powder makes you a better Mum; use a particular deodorant and you'll be a sexual hit; a box of chocolates is 'made for sharing', with all that that implies. In advertisements, magazines, television and newspapers, nudity and suggestive situations confront us daily, and the fact that most of us have to put up with second best does not in the least prevent us from striving for the ideals implied.

In time, maybe fifteen years hence, sex will have found its level and we shall be able to sit back and relax and forget that we ever felt guilty, repressed or inadequate. But for the present, sexual success, being beautiful and loved and cared for, is one of society's ideals. And in this rat-race of relationships, the deformed and the incomplete are not even in the running.

If your nose is bent you can get a new one; if you wear spectacles you can change to contact lenses; if you are fat you can diet. But if you are permanently disabled, physically or mentally, partially or severely, then to a greater or lesser degree you find yourself rejected as a non-participant. Society, by and large, just cannot cope with the idea of the disabled having the same emotional needs and desires as the rest of the population. And by society I do not mean just the ordinary able-bodied person who has little or no contact with his handicapped neighbour: what is more shocking and more serious is to find this attitude widespread amongst those who are intimately involved through their treatment and care of the disabled in their homes or in residential situations.

1

The message for too long has been: 'Sex is not for you because you are different'. The blind should worry only about seeing, and the paralysed only about walking. To occupy already troubled minds with sexual thoughts is unnecessary and unhealthy, and handicapped people who express sexual feelings are either rather disgusting and unwholesome, or comic. Hence the general practitioner who was horrified when an able-bodied woman patient with a crippled husband went to him for contraceptive advice. He could not understand why she should want it, never mind how they managed it.

Sublimation in hobbies and handicrafts, rather like cold baths for schoolboys, is supposed to take their minds off it. Yet one look at the novels written by the handicapped brings home how much they long for normal warm personal relationships, the only difference being their uncertainty about achieving them.

There is for society something disturbing about the thought of handicapped people having sexual intercourse. While 'normal' people strive more and more towards an almost unattainable ideal of sexual performance themselves, they become increasingly worried by the idea of the handicapped making love. The thought of damaged people indulging in these very intimate relationships touches off deeply personal and subconscious reactions and aversions.

This reaction is in part an expression of the feelings of the able-bodied about their own sexuality, and of their anxieties about it being dirty, disgusting or laughable. It is also unfortunately true that many people are afraid to accept that those whom they consider inferior could achieve a higher level of satisfaction than they themselves can reach. Falling short of their own standards, they find it easier to deny the disabled any right to, or need for, sexual fulfilment at all, than to accept the reality of their own sexual performance. There is often, also, the subconscious dread that the handicapped will give birth to handicapped children, and that this will in some way undermine the whole fabric of a healthy society—an assumption that is almost totally inaccurate, and totally insidious.

Yet, to take but one example, the mother who does everything for her teenage son with spina bifida, may be faced with tremendous problems if she does acknowledge his adolescent needs, rather than keeping him as a child; for in coping with his emerging sexuality she may find that she has to acknowledge a sexuality within herself that may have been submerged or repressed for many years. Hence, only too naturally, the common parental attitude of shutting one's eyes and hoping it will go away.

This is not intended as a criticism. The everyday demands made upon those who care for the disabled are tough enough as it is, and require a devotion that few outsiders would care to contemplate. However, the infantilization of developing adolescents only too often adds yet an extra strain for the young boys and girls, who, in becoming aware of their emerging sexuality, feel guilty, angry and ashamed, because they get so little help or understanding.

Many parents of *able*-bodied children fall into the same trap, and suffer the consequences. They ignore the fact that their children are growing towards adulthood, try to keep them as children, and then wonder why their daughters get pregnant and their sons sleep around. This is one of the causes of so-called sex problems among the young. If parents of disabled children refuse to acknowledge them as sexual beings, the children may use their forbidden sexuality as a weapon of adolescent rebellion like anyone else, offensively and aggressively, harming themselves and those around them.

All this is not to say that the able-bodied have sex and the handicapped have sex problems. Sex is a means of communication, and everyone has a need to communicate with other human beings in some way or other. Personal relationships of all kinds are based on communication; but the disabled, usually because of their own particular circumstances of immobility, and often living in a protected environment, have less chance than the able-bodied to make a wide circle of friends and explore and develop their feelings towards them. This is a lifelong disadvantage, affecting both the quantity and the quality of social interaction. It begins when the child is small and unable to go out and play with his peers, and continues throughout life so that the disabled miss out on all the opportunities for casual meetings and encounters, in the streets, in the discotheques, at football matches, in the club, and at work.

With fewer opportunities to meet, go fewer chances of friendship, and of learning about the needs and potentials of others; and this in its turn leads to an impoverishment in the quality of love that they are able to give.

Attitudes are changing—but slowly. What must be recognized, above all, is that if we want to bring a richer quality of life to the disabled, we must enable them to have the opportunity to love and be loved, and thus feel their worth as people. In general this has not so far been accepted as a necessary part of the caring of the disabled. There is still a conspiracy of silence, a blanket of ignorance, surrounding the emotional and sexual problems of the handicapped. Many parents and teachers, social workers and the staff of residential homes and hostels, undoubtedly meaning well, take the attitude that as sex and marriage are not for the disabled—at least in their view, and they are in a powerful decision-making role—there is no need to discuss it. In fact they are almost convinced that if they do not talk about it, it will go away, without causing any trouble. So they don't talk, and they don't give those for whom they are caring the opportunity to talk either: consequently feelings and anxieties remain bottled up, causing confusion, embarrassment and bitterness, because they can't be brought into the open, looked at and discussed, assessed or coped with.

It is here that we need to make a stand, giving young and old an opportunity to talk about their feelings, their hopes and their aspirations, and to look at their fantasies and try to match them with the reality of their situation. If we can help them to make decisions, and to take responsibility for them themselves, we shall be helping them to become bit by bit more adult and more mature.

Many disabled people will remain permanently dependent upon others; but we must realize that they have real feelings and real anxieties, and that we are doing them an injustice and a disservice by pretending that they accept their situation without anger or anguish. They are shut off from so many of the pleasures of life that the able-bodied take for granted—a walk in the rain, the luxury of privacy, of sometimes being able to get away from everybody else; the joy of picking flowers, choosing clothes; skipping, running, travelling on the top of a bus. It is because of this that we should help them to develop all possible channels of pleasure, comfort and personal fulfilment. Friendship, love and sex are all

4

pleasures. They may sometimes cause pain, but the self-exploration that is possible in a relationship with another individual is needed by everyone. They are all forms of communication and they can exist together or separately.

Friendship and love have always been valued; now gradually over the last few years we are beginning to realize that sex is as valuable a vehicle for the expression of feelings as any other. It may not be right for everyone: but everyone has the right to make their own decisions about themselves for themselves, and no one adult has the right to ride roughshod over any other, making decisions arbitrarily for him. The joy of loving another human being is an unassailable need for everyone, disabled and able-bodied alike. But because so many other pleasures are denied to them, we have a particular duty to try to help the disabled achieve a small measure of extra happiness in this area of their lives.

If we are to offer help in this direction we must be quite clear what we are offering, and to whom. Even as we use the word disabled we think of different people and different conditions, for disablement ranges from those who need total care for their very existence, to those who think of themselves as disabled because of an ugly disfigurement, or because of an inability to enjoy all the things of life that are apparently available to the able-bodied. There are those who are physically fit but mentally disabled, just as there are those who are mentally fit but physically disabled; there are those who are handicapped from birth or childhood, and those who become handicapped well into adult life or middle age.

The very way we look upon disablement, or the way we think of it, varies, depending on whether we are disabled ourselves, or are the parents of a disabled child or adult, or are in a caring or paramedical relationship to them, or are administratively responsible for the efficient running of an organization or home. And particularly are those divergencies apparent when we think about sex. Sex means quite different things to different people, from the acknowledgement of being a man or a woman, through the physical satisfactions of orgasmic relief, to the joy and comfort of being loved as an individual because we are individuals.

The aim of this book is to look at some of the problems and give the subject an airing it so badly needs. I am not

5

intending to offer outright solutions, because solutions are only appropriate after the real problem has been identified and pinpointed. Only too often the problem presented is the problem rationalized, and this may have little relevance to the reality of the situation. Increasingly, parents, teachers and social workers are wanting to know in which areas they can be of most help. Many are afraid that those in their charge may be hurt by the Permissive Society: but most appreciate that the disabled have as great a need as anyone else to experience the joy of love and sex, and realize how their lives can be enriched by it.

What this book is not doing is saying that the disabled must and can have a complete and rapturous sex life. This is after all something the able-bodied rarely have, and may not even want. Many of the problems I am going to discuss have been solved by individual disabled people themselves or by individuals caring for them; but because the subject has so many taboos attached to it, there has not been the overt discussion or the sharing of solutions that other problem areas connected with the handicapped have had.

Sex is not just a physical phenomenon. It concerns your way of life, the way you are treated, the way you react to other people and your own image of yourself as a human being, particularly when you think about attracting and being loved by a member of the opposite sex. Much of this aspect of sexual identity is rooted in our attitude towards our bodies and the way our bodies are observed and 'treated' by others. The badly disabled, who have to have so much help with their most intimate bodily needs, often never get any of that feeling of physical self-respect which is one of the bases on which sexual identity is built. Partly because of a fear of overt sexuality, and sometimes unfortunately because of a feeling among helpers that the disabled could never experience sexual feelings or arouse sexual feelings in others, they are left in a sexual limbo, knowing that they have feelings, but fearing that they are abnormal. But if they are once given the opportunity to put their thoughts into words, or to share with outsiders the secrets and secret longings they share with each other, they are found to have the same hopes and fears, the same fantasies and frustrations, the same doubts and anxieties as anyone else.

What are these sexual feelings, and how do they manifest

themselves? Sexual arousal with erection is a pleasurable recurrent part of most young men's lives, and this is heightened or relieved by masturbation for those who have little or no opportunity for sexual intercourse. Masturbation is no longer a dirty word. It is now accepted as a normal process in human physical development. The saying that ninety-nine per cent of men admit to having masturbated, and the other one per cent are liars, is a truism. Many women enjoy and practise it regularly, although possibly there are some who have less need for this form of sexual expression.

But for the disabled who have little social privacy, and sometimes not even the sheer physical ability to give themselves any type of physical pleasure or relief, the situation is quite different. The father of a thalidomide boy told me how he taught his son to masturbate; nurses and helpers 'wash' patients, or give them other help; but this is not an easy situation, and it is certainly not appropriate to expect everyone to be able to do this, however loving or caring they may be. However if parents, teachers, social workers and others in a caring role are given an opportunity to talk about their own feelings and anxieties, and their own sense of guilt, many more of them would be able to offer help.

We accept masturbation as part of the 'growing up' process of the able-bodied youngster, and hope that he will eventually grow through this and achieve an inter-personal sexual relationship which gives not only the physical pleasure, but emotional satisfactions too. How then does this fit into our picture of the handicapped? Unfortunately, society still pays lip-service to the restriction of sexual satisfaction to the marriage relationship. This is fine for those lucky enough to find a suitable partner; but more and more people are asking why physical satisfaction should be denied to those who either do not wish to marry or are not fortunate enough to meet the right person. We have consequently reached a state in which society accepts that adults should be allowed to do what they want, but still feels that the young should be protected from themselves as far as possible. The handicapped of whatever age come into the same category as the young: they have to be protected, often without any questioning whether what they are being protected from is really all that dangerous.

Of course there are dangers. No one would pretend that the dangers do not exist. But allowing individuals sometimes to make decisions for themselves, taking risks and understanding the implications of their actions, can help them to grow as people. Being over-protective is never kind, and is often cruel. And although there are dangers, they are perhaps not quite so bad as we imagine. Unwanted pregnancy, for example, today need never be a problem; and in this context, the risk of venereal disease is on the whole much less high than in the community in general. The problem of exploitation is a much more serious one; but feelings between the able-bodied and the disabled are not necessarily unhealthy, and most of us if we are completely honest with ourselves, would rather have loved and lost, than never have loved at all.

There are two main factors which thwart any sexual expression by the disabled. One is the belief among those of us in a caring role that perhaps it is all wrong and sinful—although if we are honest with ourselves we might admit that these feelings are at least partly based on our own feelings of inadequacy, and our need to bolster ourselves by believing that another group performs less well than we do. The other factor is the appalling lack of privacy that most disabled people have to put up with. Few residential homes have double rooms. They are mostly very small singles or dormitories, neither of which is conducive to the sort of exploration of self and others that is usually an accepted part of normal life. Some couples have to do their courting in bathrooms, or through the windows of invalid cars. This is the only way they can be alone. How far any couple can experiment together depends only too often on the attitude of parents and residential staffs; and although it is often adults they are looking after, they are not sure whether they should allow them to behave like adults in this way. This is partly because of their own inhibitions, and partly due to the fact that they are afraid of not being able to control the situation once they open the floodgates. What makes things worse is the dependence of the disabled because of lack of transport and limited mobility. They cannot just go out and get a bus. They have to rely on others for every move outside they make.

It is only too easy for the handicapped to believe themselves unlovable because of their disability, and for their

8

feelings of rejection to be constantly reinforced because they seem to be barred from the world of physical love. And let us not forget that these feeling of rejection, along with many of the sex problems, are due above all to the difficulties of transportation and the lack of opportunity to mix socially. Obviously the disabled do suffer from sexual difficulties such as frigidity and impotence; but whether or not these problems are greater, or more severe, than those similarly suffered by the able-bodied, is unknown. What is clear though is that it is very easy for anyone to blame his shortcomings on real or imagined disability; but whereas the able-bodied can turn to the counselling agencies, this is not so easy for the disabled. Counselling is still a bit of a Cinderella, and services provided either by voluntary organizations or by statutory authorities are often found at the top of a flight of stairs or in another town out of the reach of anyone in a wheelchair or without independent transport.

As long as we deny the sex feelings of the disabled, we inhibit them from being able to ask for help. But they do have sex feelings, and they do, like anyone else, have problems; and because they have problems they need help—far more help than is available at present.

There is also a need for more tolerance towards those disabled people who want to form homosexual relationships and may want help in examining their feelings.

Those who become disabled later in life are probably given more help than most, although distressingly large numbers are given no sexual counselling at all. Many men have great anxiety about their sexual future and their ability to fulfil conjugal obligations, and a distressingly high proportion of marriages break down after the disablement of one partner. We still tend to equate manliness with sexual performance, and when that suddenly ceases, doubts are also cast upon the man's ability to play his traditional role in the family and in society.

A woman's role and her femininity often depend on her ability to be a wife and a mother. If we allow the handicapped to love and be loved do we then allow them to marry and have children? This is one of the greatest dilemmas, and although marriage in itself may be acceptable, society's feelings towards this are still so mixed that accommodation for the disabled couple is only half-heartedly provided. Parents are often very ambivalent. If their handicapped child can marry someone who will look after him or her, then it doesn't seem so bad, even though many mothers of handicapped children doubt if anyone can care for their child as they do. But at the idea of one handicapped person marrying another, many parents are shocked, forgetting that the rough and tumble of ordinary living, when shared with a loving companion, can be a journey of personal enrichment and spiritual fulfilment. If we treat individuals as adults they usually behave like adults. But up till now our treatment of the handicapped has not been that of one adult to another: we have tended to adopt the hot-house principle of care. There are of course some parents and residential staffs who have long recognized the handicapped person's right to have a say in his own destiny, to live and to love as he wants. But they are rare.

So I am not setting out in this book to make people dissatisfied with what they have got. Nor am I attempting to give the disabled more information so that they can more fully appreciate what they are missing. The aim is to point out that the handicapped have a right to love and be loved, and a right to be hurt. This is part of the human condition. At present a large section of the community is 'keeping them out of it'. This is well meaning, but ultimately grossly unfair.

2

The handicapped adolescent and sex

There is a danger, in discussing the sex problems of the disabled, of implying that people with physical and mental disabilities are also sexually handicapped, and consequently in yet another way 'different' and separate from the rest of society. There are enough myths around to support this theory: that the handicapped have insatiable sexual appetites from which we must all be protected, that deviation is rife, with its associated horrors of witchcraft, unnatural practices and contamination. To which your average handicapped person will probably reply: 'I should be so lucky!'

The sex problems that the handicapped face are only different in that for too long society has not credited them even with the *capacity* for falling in and out of love, for feeling sexual urges, for wanting emotional satisfaction, marriage and even children. This denial of basic human needs starts in the cradle. Many parents make a judgment upon their child as soon as the extent of the disability is known; from that moment, partly because they believe the child will never marry, partly because of understandable feelings of pity, and partly because the very thought of the future is frightening, there is a temptation to keep the child neuter, sexless.

From the highest motives, and with an intimate knowledge that he will suffer enough just through being handicapped, they attempt to shield the child from the ordinary unpleasant and unhappy things of life. But they forget that this is how every child learns to live, by being exposed to hurt. If a child, any child, is protected from pain, tears and rejection, he is missing a vital part of the growing-up process; and he is missing the satisfaction of knowing that he can bear the pain and come out the other side, not necessarily smiling but a

11

little more mature and complete as a human being. Every child must fall from his bicycle and bleed, fight for a friend and come home crying, be reprimanded by a teacher and bear a grudge. But to say to a child, 'you are a two-dimensional being and we feel it our duty to safeguard you from this third dimension of experience because you would not be able to cope', is to deny that child the right to develop into an individual, into an adult, with the ability to give back something to society instead of always being on the receiving end of charity and care, always expressing gratitude without really being grateful.

This is where sexual awareness can play a significant part in the life of the young handicapped adolescent. First, though, it must be reiterated that what we are talking about when we discuss sex and disability is not how to have intercourse in a wheelchair or how to flirt in an invalid car. It is the wider approach of integrity and humanity, and the questions of how the disabled person sees himself and how sex can enrich his life and enrich society at the same time. That is the extra dimension.

Many disabled people feel cut off from society, outcasts from ordinary experience, protected from the darker side of life, mixing only with those similarly handicapped. And these feelings are reinforced when parents and others who care for them imply that sex is not for them, and do everything to avoid arousing emotional and sexual urges. 'They don't have the same feelings as other people, and anyway marriage is out of the question, so what's the point?' This attitude is based on the belief that what you do not have you do not miss—which may apply to caviar and smoked salmon, but not to sex. Apart from the fact that sex is undeniably good for you, this proposition ignores the emphasis that society is currently placing on it through advertising, television, books and magazines, which constantly thrust it at us with the certain intent of arousing and titillating. The handicapped youngster sees as much of this as anyone, perhaps more, if he is housebound with time on his hands.

When we talk about the handicapped youngster we are embracing a group of children who are suffering from congenital disabilities from birth, like spina bifida and cerebral palsy; a not inconsiderable group with Friedrich's ataxia, muscular dystrophy, or illnesses which develop during

12

early adolescence; children who are injured as a result of car accidents; the children with retarded growth; the blind, the deaf, and epileptics. On top of which there are the mentally retarded, who may have an even greater feeling of alienation from society.

How society views the handicapped varies little whether they are physically or mentally disabled. There is possibly more sympathy and understanding for the deaf and the blind, mainly because these disabilities do not always create disfigurement, but also perhaps because it is easier to imagine what it would be like to be sightless or without hearing. But by and large they are all grouped together in society's mind as separate and 'special'. How they cope depends entirely on their upbringing.

A large number live at home until their adolescence, when caring for a growing child becomes too difficult for parents who may be aging (and there is a high incidence of disability among children born to older mothers). It is relatively easy to bath and dress a five-year-old, but later it becomes a tremendous strain; so there are peaks when children move into residential care. This is not always simply because parents can no longer easily provide the care; they feel that the child will benefit from community living, and they are also looking to the future when they will no longer be around to care for him.

On the whole children do better if they are kept at home as long as the family can help the child to grow, rather than simply protect and care for him. But there is a tragically large number of children at home who still have one or other parent dressing and bathing them, when in fact with the right encouragement and patience they would be able to do it themselves. This is part of the infantilization process. A member of staff of a newly opened hostel for spastics told me that a high proportion of the new arrivals in their early 20s had never done this basic daily routine for themselves; extra staff had to be brought in to cope, but when over the following few months they were encouraged to do these small tasks for themselves, much less supervision was needed. A Swedish report on handicapped children at home and in care tells of a boy of 17 who was sent to a boarding school and only then discovered for the first time that he really did have a chance with girls. At home he had been so shy and depressed that he dared not approach a girl even if the girl showed interest. At school he discovered that he could compete successfully with other boys.

This is undoubtedly how children learn to live and grow, through their everyday experiences and through contact with their peers at school and in the street. Under normal circumstances able-bodied children usually have two sets of friends to relate to: those they mix with in the classroom and the playground, and, depending on how far away from school they live, a completely different set around their home. At school and at home they are supervised to a certain extent; but somewhere between the two they manage to be exclusively among their contemporaries, testing out their strengths and their weaknesses with passionate friendships and violent feuds. They fight and tease and touch each other, groping and feeling each others' bodies and beginning to recognize the signals of pleasure and indifference and animosity. As they grow older they hold hands, dance together, sit close on chairs, push and shove and generally indulge in the socially acceptable exploration of feelings and reactions which is their early introduction to sexual excitement and awareness. It is a perfectly healthy part of growing up, which parents may condone to a greater or lesser degree depending on their own backgrounds and attitudes. In any case, children have plenty of opportunity for all these formative activities away from the critical gaze of parents and teachers.

This is where the handicapped child misses out. Parents or supervisors will deliver to, and fetch from, school, making street play in between with children of his own age impossible. He returns immediately to the protected environment of the home, without friends, and possibly with brothers and sisters who treat him—again from the highest motives of love—like a precious object with kid-glove care. Parents exercise the caring and concerned authority over the disabled child which they are not able to maintain over the ordinary adolescent, who has the freedom to come and go as he pleases, to answer back, to rebel, in fact to be independent—an adult in the making.

The mother of an able-bodied 15-year-old girl may want to see her to the bus stop at night and collect her from a party; but there comes a time when the teenager calls a halt to this

14

supervision, and the parent, however unwillingly, has to agree to take the risk she alone sees, and trust her daughter. But the mother of a handicapped teenager always has a good reason to oversee his or her activities. The boy or girl has few opportunities of being alone with a contemporary of the opposite sex to discuss private thoughts, to touch and to grope and to experience the basic human needs of love and warmth.

The handicapped youngster is also at the mercy of his parents' standards and morals, and rarely has the chance to find out that his contemporaries may be behaving quite differently with a new set of values. There is also the feeling among some parents that if their son or daughter is to have boy-friends and girl-friends they should only develop stable, steady relationships and not chop and change, which is the accepted behaviour of most teenagers. The reason for this is the fear that if they swop around they will risk getting hurt; and being more hurt than is necessary is what they must be protected from.

It may be permissible for them to kiss and hold hands; but parents may deliberately prevent the relationship going any further, on the grounds that, as marriage is not going to be possible, then sex must not be allowed to rear its ugly head. A young disabled couple told me that they had been courting innocently for a few years, when the club they belonged to organized a group holiday in Belgium. The girl's parents put their foot down and prevented her going because, so she discovered later, they feared that she and her boy-friend might take the opportunity to sleep together and that she might get pregnant. Then the question of marriage might come up. At the time, however, they simply said they did not want her to go because of the problems with getting in and out of the aeroplane.

The significant point is that parents of the disabled desperately want their children to marry someone who will be able to look after their offspring when they are gone. And it is characteristic of the parents in the story above that they hang on to their daughter in the hope that something better will turn up for her. Yet this likelihood is unrealistic and remote, so they are denying two people a real chance of satisfying their tremendous urge to love and care for each other. Marriage for two people like this *can* be rewarding.

15

Even if there is a chance that one partner will die prematurely, the other will have had a few years of happiness that no one can take away.

The handicapped child often grows up with a rather peculiar attitude towards his body. Because he is often in and out of hospitals and clinics at an early age, as specialists try to improve his condition, other people are constantly handling his body; he is touched and manipulated in private places and personal ways, which the able-bodied patient would not have to tolerate, and certainly would not accept. Those who are fit and well develop a skin around them which is usually only breached when they are in an emotional relationship with someone else, and when the personal touching, in which each is touching as well as being touched, is part of that relationship. For example a husband scrubs his wife's back in the bath, or a girl puts her hand on her boyfriend's knee; but if you accidentally brush against someone in a bus queue you always apologize.

The handicapped person is being handled—for impersonal, unemotional and probably professional reasons—without apology, and therefore develops a quite different, sometimes oddly objective, attitude towards his body. He might perhaps therefore be less sensitive to the approach of someone of the opposite sex. Yet in making this assumption I am implying that what the able-bodied person feels is somehow superior in quality; and that would be falling into the same trap that this book is trying to challenge, of separating the feelings of the handicapped from those of the able-bodied and saying they are inferior.

How you react to certain situations does depend on the sum of your experiences. If handicapped people have been prevented from going through this period of groping and caressing, with all that it subtly implies, and have instead become used to being handled in a cold professional way by doctors and strangers, then they have missed a valuable part of the growing process and of becoming aware of themselves and others. This perception of themselves, as desirable or otherwise, conditions to a certain extent their expectations of themselves and other people's expectations of them. The able-bodied adolescent girl who believes herself to be ugly does not go out of her way to make herself beautiful; just the reverse, she perversely reinforces her feelings of inferiority to

16

convince herself that she is right. Underneath she may well be dreaming of marrying a pop star, just as the handicapped youngster dreams of marrying an able-bodied partner. Both situations are relatively unlikely; but with the handicapped child this fantasy may last longer.

So how can a parent, friend or mentor help the disabled youngster grow through these fantasies and get to grips with reality without actually dampening his or her spirits, hopes and desires? They can undoubtedly help by discussing fantasy and reality frankly and openly, so that the young can put into words their fears and hopes, preferably in company with their contemporaries both handicapped and able-bodied. The more opportunity the disabled child has to meet contemporaries, the better he will be able to face the reality of his life. He will see that all adolescents have problems, and that this period of life is full of sexual frustration for everyone. A healthy dialogue with friends of his own age will cut through any endeavours on the part of parents to cover up the truth. Children are piercingly honest with each other. Their peers do not allow them to be otherwise. For this reason there is a strong argument in favour of allowing the not-too-handicapped child to attend an ordinary school. Obviously the severely handicapped need the specialized care of the special school, but the integration of the handicapped where possible with their able-bodied contemporaries would enrich the experience of both. Society is after all made up of the weak and the strong, and school is a reflection of the community in its cross-section of types and abilities. This is the principle of comprehensive schooling, and could be taken a stage further in practice.

Society is beginning to come round to the idea that sex should not be denied those for whom marriage is not possible. Today we no longer eat simply to keep body and soul together, according to the Puritan ethic; we enjoy food as a pleasure. With sex it is the same. We are accepting that it is not just a reproductive process but a means of self-expression and communication. I would not recommend a hedonistic snatching of brief moments of pleasure, because there is more to sex than jumping from one bed to another. But the disabled should have the same opportunities as the able-bodied to know, not just the physical release of tension that sexual intercourse brings, but also the sharing, the loving

17

and being loved, and the closeness. They should be helped to see their bodies not as a hindrance, but as a source of pleasure. This is not always easy, especially for those with painful disfigurements. But one of the aims of counselling might be, for example, to help teenage girls to understand that personality and warmth are more important than a pretty face and a pair of sexy legs.

A disabled woman in her early twenties told me after an affair was over: 'The fact that I was loved for myself regardless of how I looked helped me to forget my disability. It took away my self-pity and put self-respect in its place. Being handicapped was less important than being loved and loving. It didn't last, but I don't regret a minute of it.' This woman found herself for the first time taking an interest in her clothes, her make-up, her finger nails, just as a scruffy teenage boy suddenly gets smartened up for his first date.

This is yet another aspect of the denial of sexuality: the drabness of the disabled. Another disabled woman told me: 'When I was young I was positively discouraged from looking nice, or making anything of myself. I always had hand-me-downs. No one told me that plumage and colour were to attract others. I suppose my mother had a vested interest in keeping me dowdy, and I did too. I can see now that deep down I was defending myself from the outside world, keeping them away by being unattractive. I believed that there was no point dressing up because where would it get me?' So she continued to reinforce her feelings of inferiority.

A lot of disabled people are afraid of their sexuality because they have not been given licence to use it. They are afraid of arousing their own feelings. One worker in a residential unit tells of the couples in their 30s who will sit for hours holding hands, still frightened of the feelings they might arouse in each other because their knowledge of sex is all based on myth and moral prejudice, like little girls who tell each other that kissing makes you pregnant.

Yet the handicapped are subjected to the same stimulation from the media as anyone else, and learn from magazines and films what is the current ideal of manhood and womanhood. They know only too well that they have little chance of matching up to it, so this just succeeds in underlining their feelings of inadequacy. They have been told on countless occasions that they have no chance of sexual fulfilment, so

18

they retreat behind a veneer of drabness; and this barrier applies not only to outward appearances but to their personality too. There is no point in being sparkling and effervescent, because where does it get you? It just emphasizes your inability to compete.

Ann Shearer, in a study of this subject for the Spastics Society, wrote: '. . . we make sure in our financial, physical and social provision for (the handicapped) that they will find it hard to express their feelings. We deny them the fulfilment of marriage and children on the grounds that they could not cope; yet we would be properly horrified if anyone suggested that the children of broken homes, or people on low wages, should be barred from marriage.'

The sheer physical problems of transport and mobility can easily prevent a handicapped person overcoming the first hurdle, of communication with the opposite sex. The provision of invalid cars was at first a humane gesture, but it has turned out to be unexpectedly anti-social. A young man with a damaged spine came to me recently. He had quite a good job which made him financially independent, and an invalid car which made him mobile. He said he had no problems finding girls to go out with; but because of his one-seater car he always had to meet them in the cinema or theatre, and afterwards they would have to go their separate ways before meeting again in a bar or café. Any romantic contact he might have got going in the cinema was destroyed by the parting of the ways, and he had to start again at their next rendezvous. His great aim was to save for an ordinary car that he could have adapted.

A disabled girl in her late teens, who was dating a man a little older, told me with great humour but not without a tinge of sadness how they drove their separate invalid cars to a seaside rendezvous to look at the sea and the stars. They would park them close enough to gaze into each other's eyes and hold hands through the windows. 'Fortunately we were able to see the funny side of it, but I guess it was even more comic to those watching,' she said. Had they been able to share a car none of this embarrassment would have arisen, and they could have gone courting with the same privacy everyone else takes for granted. A young couple with less resilience probably would not have been able to put up with the stares of onlookers.

The difficulties of getting around loom very large in the everyday life of the disabled, and mean that they have to plan their social and sexual activities more carefully and less spontaneously than the rest of us. Here then are strong and already well documented arguments in favour of invalid cars for two, or grants for the modification of ordinary cars.

The young disabled person is so indoctrinated in the denial of his sexuality that when he does feel a sexual urge it produces feelings of guilt and shame. Because he has been told he cannot and will not have sexual feelings he imagines that what he is in fact feeling is abnormal, and his guilt in turn stops him seeking counselling advice. He probably considers it a problem to be borne in silence and not openly discussed, rather like sex in the Victorian age.

One of these areas of guilt for both the adolescent and society around him is the question of masturbation. For many disabled people this will be the only aspect of sexual activity they can ever enjoy for the physical release of tension, either because intercourse is physically impossible or because no partner turns up. But if such a person is overwhelmed by feelings of guilt every time he or she masturbates, then its benefit is reduced and the frustration increased. To be able to talk about masturbation as a perfectly normal sexual function that does not, as the old myth would have it, make you go blind, will considerably help in alleviating the guilt.

The mother of a handicapped child told me of the first time she 'caught', to use her own words, her son masturbating. She was horrified and ran to her husband. He told her quietly to turn her back 'because our son was learning a skill'. He suggested that her only involvement be making sure the boy could reach for the paper tissues to clean up after him so that parents need not be involved.

The blind adolescent often has all these problems and more. Communication is the first step to a relationship, and without sight it is almost impossible to know how someone is reacting to your signals. The way people sit, the expression on their faces, the action of their hands—this is the language on which relationships are based. So much is expressed without words. This problem is perhaps less acute for two blind people, helped by the knowledge that neither can see, than for a couple where only one is blind. But there is

20

another problem, that the blind are not so aware of what is acceptable behaviour in society. The spastic or the child with spina bifida will have seen what people do and do not do, even if they cannot join in. Today couples kiss and hug in the street; but a blind person will not know just how far it is socially permissible to go. This applies to masturbation. Just as one might have the urge to itch, one might feel like masturbating; but the sighted know that this is not done in public, although nobody actually spells it out to them. And since if you are blind, even if your other senses are well developed, you do not always know when you are 'in public', or being watched, your sense of privacy is distorted.

Even where the disability, as with epilepsy for example, is not immediately evident to the outsider, the sufferer can be faced with enormous psychological problems of rejection, which diminish him in his own eyes if not in other people's. Epilepsy is unusual in this respect: the scientific advances which enable the epileptic to live a normal life have created a new problem. When it was less easy to control attacks, fits were more frequent, and friends, family and colleagues became accustomed to them and could cope. Today they are rarely seen and therefore, when they do happen, are more frightening to the onlooker.

All these disabilities are equally devastating, whether they are nothing more than a strawberry mark, or are all-consuming like total paralysis. Either way the disabled person justifiably—because of society's attitude—feels underprivileged. There is no reason why society's increasing tolerance and understanding in other areas should not extend to the vital enriching area of sexuality, and every reason to hope that it will.

The picture of the accepting, grateful cripple, who gladly settles for having no sex feelings and sits back humbly and patiently in his wheelchair, while the rest of the world gets on with its sexual acrobatics, is a fantasy in the mind of the outside world. The reality of the situation is that the physically and mentally handicapped are not necessarily sexually handicapped. Given opportunities and support, they can begin to give as well as to receive.

21

3

Marriage (1)

One of the most telling remarks made by a handicapped person came from a spastic, married to an equally badly handicapped wife. 'For as long as I can remember,' he wrote, 'I have been conscious of two me's—the outer casing which is visible to the world and the inner substance which is not. The outer casing is of course my body and is the façade by which in all but a few circumstances the world judges me. The inner part is my mind, my character, my conscience and my true being. Take away my twisted limbs, peel off my peculiar facial expressions and remove all traces of my athetoid condition and you will be left with a normal man.' Presumably it was the qualities of the 'normal' man that his wife first perceived—and vice versa—that enabled them to fall in love and marry.

Unfortunately for many handicapped people the 'normal' man or woman within them, the real self, is suppressed and forced to give way to the all-consuming disabled body or mind which the world sees and too readily judges. First impressions are lasting—and yet ugly women still find husbands, and overweight men lovers. On any day of the week in any street you see couples contentedly walking arm in arm, and you wonder what they see in each other and how they ever came to link their lives together. The answer is that the man with the obese wife sees through the layers of fat to the individual inside, to the real person she is, capable of loving and being loved. He may not like her being fat; but he married her for what she is, not what she looks like.

A lot of women write to me complaining that if only their breasts were bigger their husbands would love them more. This is nonsense, because they could have the cleavage of a beauty queen and their men would still find something to criticize. Their feelings about their inadequate proportions are only a symptom of something much deeper. No one is perfect, and the happiest marriages are between people who realize this, recognize each other's limitations and can express and accept their mutual feelings of inadequacy and their particular needs and anxieties. Communication is the key word in any discussion on relationships, sex and marriage; because the ability to put those very personal feelings into words and deeds, not only helps a couple to understand and appreciate each other, but also helps *them* to grow as individuals, and the marriage to develop into something worthwhile and lasting.

Where many marriages go wrong—particularly among the young—is in ignoring the fact that communication is not only communicating one's strong points. It is showing that there are weaknesses and vulnerable spots too. For the disabled contemplating marriage, the fear of being unlovable is reinforced by the fear that if they reveal their weaknesses they may seem even less attractive. If they go into marriage concealing their real emotional needs and bottling up frustrations and depressions and putting a brave face on it, they will be heading for trouble. It is knowing that you will be loved warts and all that makes marriage a rewarding experience. No marriage can survive on false pretences, and I believe this is why marriage for the handicapped is such a contentious subject.

Marriage for the handicapped falls into three different categories. There is marriage between two disabled people, whether of equal or differing degrees of disablement; there is marriage between an able-bodied person and someone disabled; and there is marriage between two able-bodied people one of whom becomes disabled later through a sudden accident or illness. And there is no doubt that as more and more handicapped people begin to be integrated into society through jobs and more opportunities to travel, more will contemplate marriage. Economic independence and the need to be part of the real world will all make this possible.

Society may look upon the disabled as sexless objects, rather than as men and women of flesh and blood, but it seems to be able to accept more easily the idea of marriage if it is between two disabled people. The spastic whose quotation opened this chapter has written of his neighbours' reactions when he and his new wife moved into their bungalow: 'They gave us strange looks at first and I was asked once or twice how my sister was, and hawkers would ask if my father was at home. But when it was seen that we lived quite ordinary lives we were accepted.' How qualified this acceptance can be, however, was sadly and succinctly described by a woman with severe rheumatoid arthritis, who said that society's feeling of repugnance for the disabled is 'not apparent when two invalids marry each other. As long as they keep to themselves society does not seem to mind. The invalid may marry another of his kind and live happily ever after. Society doesn't really care . . . as long as society is not troubled. A wall is raised between the "normal" world and the world of the disabled, a wall invisible and hard and cold as unbreakable glass.'

When a young handicapped person contemplates marriage, his first stumbling block is usually parental opposition. From the best of motives, parents feel that another handicapped person cannot look after their 'child' as well as they can. After all they have devoted their lives to the care of their handicapped child and know instinctively his every need. But parents can be ambivalent and may be objecting to the marriage for selfish reasons, because they really want to keep their child at home. Devoted care of this vulnerable human being may have become their way of life, to the exclusion of all other interests. If that child wants to leave them for another, less capable person, their feelings of rejection can be very acute: they feel that all their efforts in the past have been wasted, and that their lives will be empty. Equally they may genuinely fear for the child's well-being, without understanding that physical well-being is not the most important thing in life, especially to a young person in love. Parents in their middle years often take the attitude that their needs are also their children's needs. You see this when parents disapprove of their kids going camping in wet fields instead of spending a holiday with them in a comfortable hotel. Yet the standards we set ourselves are not the standards of others. After all many young couples go from their parents' comfortable semi-detached house with central heating and colour television into cold and damp bedsitters when they marry. They do not particularly care. They are willing to go without certain creature comforts when they are in love and happy, because part of building a marriage is building a home, starting from scratch and making sacrifices along the way.

Parents of the handicapped are often in the same way pessimistic about the couple's ability to cope with everyday problems and tasks. What happens when the roof leaks or there's a fire in the kitchen? Will they be vulnerable to the overtures of persistent door-to-door salesmen, and less likely to be able to run for help in an emergency? These are all valid fears. And parents sometimes feel they will have to take the blame if anything does go wrong. Yet how a couple cope will depend on the level of independence they have been allowed to develop as they grew up, on whether they were given the chance to mature into adults or were shielded from making their own decisions and experiencing crises.

Disabled young people should be allowed to take these risks, and be given the same chances as others to learn that marriage is a growing process that does not stand still once the licence has been taken out. Happy marriages do not happen miraculously. As with any friendship, both partners have to put in a great deal in order to take anything out, if it is to be a good marriage. The same principles apply for the disabled as the able-bodied. So if things are made too easy for the disabled couple, if all the problems of running a home are ironed out for them, if they are not allowed to share the same everyday traumas and problems as everyone else at the beginning of marriage, whether it be making do with two chairs and a table, arguing over the wife's cooking, or saving to pay the bills, they may never get a potentially viable marriage off the ground. Some of the most successful marriages are those in which the couple have to share early hardship. The ones that crumble are often those built on a bed of roses.

The tragedy is that those parents who oppose marriage for their handicapped son or daughter are more likely to be those who have protected them from becoming adults, so that they probably *are* in consequence less able than they might be to lead an independent life, not just physically but emotionally. This is not to say that the more independent young handicapped person has no problems when he leaves home and attempts to break the umbilical cord: he may not have realized just how much he relied on them, even though he

25

was free to come and go, drive his own car, have his own friends.

One young man I met in a hostel for the handicapped, who worked in a sheltered workshop, told me he was planning to marry a handicapped girl. They were going to try and find themselves a flat outside, and he would change his job to a factory or office so that he could earn more money. At the time he was having everything done for him at the hostel, his meals were put in front of him on time, his washing miraculously reappeared clean every week, and he never had to concern himself with dripping taps or an overgrown garden. I do not think he realized either, that life in a busy office or factory might be more hectic and cut-throat than in the workshop. Clashes of personality, ambition, office politics, union pressures—all these things would be new to him. His wife might find it difficult to get the dinner on time, have a clean shirt ready every morning and keep the house clean. I felt, and I told him, that they were going to have to face tremendous personal crises and develop an enormous amount of mutual understanding of each other's limitations if the marriage was going to work.

He was confident that all would be well. However there are many handicapped couples who really do worry that they may make a mess of things. I know of one woman who turned down a genuine offer of marriage, because she had been brought up to believe that marriage meant being a good housewife and she knew she would not be. There are other worries: a handicapped couple have so much more to lose if the marriage fails. For the able-bodied there is often a second chance, a new partner, a new job, if they want it. They can move to another part of the country, bury themselves in a new interest. Things do not work out so simply for the disabled because they have not the freedom of choice or movement. The only alternative for most would be a return to the home or hostel or back to parents; and it takes a very mature person to accept defeat gracefully under these circumstances and come out smiling.

A spastic couple who married against their parents' wishes and moved into a small flat, came near to breaking point just after the weeding. They felt their parents' eyes were watching their every move for a mistake to justify their opposition, and they found it took them much longer to get things done

26

in the house than they had expected. Housework which the girl had never really had to do before was the main bone of contention; they started bickering, and this led to serious arguments. Resentments came to the surface, and they made it plain to each other that this was not the life they had hoped for. By a stroke of good fortune they had a marriage guidance counsellor living across the landing from them; she had been friendly from the start, so the girl poured out her troubles to her. With her help they began to weigh up the reality of the situation against their expectations—the husband could not expect his wife to run the house as efficiently as his mother had, and she saw that he was never going to be a great do-it-yourself expert, and it would all take time.

This couple clearly had a vested interest in making the marriage work and, more important, were able to express their feelings. It is when feelings of hostility and anger and frustration are either suppressed or wrongly interpreted that the trouble starts. Bottled-up resentment develops into anger, which then turns in on itself, causing severe depresson. This of course can happen to any married couple, and is a major cause of depression among married women today. But with a disabled couple it can be more destructive.

There is a feeling among the able-bodied that two handicapped people who live together are doubling their problems rather than halving them. But if you consider this logically the reverse must be true. What society has to do for one disabled person, it can do for two together; and by providing one roof over two heads and helping two people help each other, it can surely alleviate many of the economic problems. This is not to deny that life for the handicapped can be very expensive: homes, gadgets, transport, all have to be adapted for particular needs. But it still makes economic sense to house the handicapped in specially adapted accommodation and then allow them the chance to live independent of society, rather than keep them at the State's expense for the rest of their lives in an institution.

A Spastics Society report had this to say on the question of housing for the handicapped: 'Clearly the degree of the couple's handicap will dictate to some extent the kind of house with which they can cope. For some, a ground floor flat in a normal housing estate will be enough; but councils are not always awake to the needs of the handicapped—who

27

will be very often unlikely to earn enough to buy their own house—when planning housing. Others may need sheltered housing, and some voluntary bodies are now planning flatlets attached to their hostels. But most handicapped people, where possible, will want an independent home. Sheltered housing groups in the centre of populations are the best solution here. But one proposal that most handicapped people would reject completely is that of the "village" or "colony" of similarly handicapped people.'

An ideal alternative, still unfortunately a long way from being realized, is care within the community—where the old and the disabled and the underprivileged can be part of that community as well as the fit and able. This may sound Utopian; but it is in fact much more realistic to integrate weaker members of the community to the mutual benefit of all. The disabled can then begin to give something back to society rather than always being on the receiving end; at the very least they can babysit and take messages for instance. The benefit for the able members of the community is in learning at first hand that there are other people who have to be considered.

At present there are other practical problems facing the handicapped when they go into marriage. There are the questions of whether they will cope financially, what grants are available, whether they can do certain things for each other that they had done for them in the past. But the people involved in caring for the disabled often report that they do much better than everyone expects. All they need is the incentive; and the rewards of marriage often provide just that.

Society finds it less easy to accept the concept of a fit and healthy person marrying someone disabled. Here is another quote from the Spastics Society report: 'A young man severely handicapped and bound to a wheelchair who recently married a non-handicapped wife, tells of a couple down the block from them who referred to him as "the gentleman we've seen you with" when they met his wife. The word husband was too strong for them. Acquaintances try to put a martyr's crown on her—why else would such a nice girl have taken on such a man? Their GP, when the wife asked for contraceptive advice, was horrified. You don't mean to say you have sexual relations with him? The same man notices a furious resentment of his marriage in some able-bodied men. Is it too much of a challenge to their own marriages? Could *they* keep the loyalty of a wife if, like him, they did not support the household, could not do a man's work around the place?'

The principal problem for a marriage between an able-bodied person and someone handicapped is one of motivation. It begs the cruel and unavoidable question: 'What normal person would saddle him/herself with someone who will probably need a lifetime of care?' Many 'normal' people when they enter a marriage of this nature are not marrying an equal but someone they want to treat like a child.

A typical example is the girl who followed her mother into nursing. She was one of five children, the father was very much the boss and was a violent and unpredictable bully. After a couple of years' nursing the girl met and married a patient, a paraplegic. She told me at the time that at the back of her mind was the thought that her husband would never be able to behave towards her as her father had towards her mother. She was in fact protecting herself.

Obviously motivation of pity or self-protection does not always apply. Certainly not in the case of the childhood sweethearts who took it for granted that they would one day marry, until after a six-month engagement the girl was found to be suffering from multiple sclerosis. The young man was taken on one side and told that his girl friend would always need looking after and that he should reconsider his position. No one would really blame him if he broke it off, he was told. His answer was that he had always envisaged life with this girl and nothing had changed this view.

Some handicapped adolescents, particularly boys, feel very strongly that they want a 'whole' partner. They think, for one thing, that that would make them feel and seem less handicapped. They are also hoping that one day they too may be 'whole'. Neither of these reasons is really very realistic. One of the hazards is that if the able-bodied partner has been motivated into marriage by pity or the desire to care for the weaker partner, then the handicapped person may find him/herself making love to a mother or father figure. That the 'whole' partner may conversely be making love to someone he or she is caring for as a child, only makes the situation more dangerous. The feelings may only be subconscious, or barely recognized for what they are, but they can still produce nasty hang-ups. The point is that marriage is something that happens between equals, and a couple need to grow together to achieve a satisfactory adult relationship.

Another problem is that the handicapped (say) husband may begin to resent his unavoidable dependence. His gratitude and joy subtly change to anger as he starts believing that his wife married him not for the man he is but to care for him regardless of whether he needs care all the time or not. Or it may be that the man no longer needs as much care as he did, but the wife still insists on caring for him in this maternal way rather than allowing herself to love him as an adult for himself. If a couple in this way do not grow and alter in parallel, recognizing and adapting to their changing needs, there may well be tension in the marriage, and problems in bed.

An obstacle which is often put in the way of a marriage of this kind is the suggestion that the disabled partner may die prematurely. This is of course an unhappy possibility, especially with such diseases as multiple sclerosis. But the harsh reality of the situation is that the one left behind may not be any worse off after the bereavement than if he or she had not married at all; they both will probably, with the right motivation, have gained a great deal from the relationship, and those few years of happiness may be worth the loneliness that follows bereavement.

Now we come to the marriage where disablement has occurred at a later stage, and this presents a whole new set of tragic circumstances. Many marriages break down under the strain of one partner becoming totally dependent on the other—although occasionally the opposite happens and the tragedy can strengthen what may previously have been a rather creaky relationship.

There is a sadly high separation rate recorded for when a serious road-accident has maimed one of the partners, involving perhaps spinal injury or brain damage. Separation is, perhaps understandably, most prevalent where the wife has become disabled. At a hospital dealing with many spinal injuries as a result of car accidents social workers say that at the time of the accident families tend to rally round and put a brave face on things; but when the reality of the future pattern of life becomes clear, the strain on the relationship begins to tell, and many marriages break down or slowly disintegrate.

It is very easy to see how this happens, and anyone who contemplates the problem must shudder to think how he would react in the same circumstances. Indeed, this identification often makes other people unusually tolerant of marriage breakdown, where for instance a man leaves his newly crippled wife. When it is the man, the breadwinner, who has become disabled, everything changes and everyone in the family has to change. The man has to re-think his role in the family, not just from the practical point of view of balancing the budget, but adjusting psychologically to being no longer the head of the household, the decision maker. Today, even despite a shifting of roles, the man, the father and husband, still takes many of the major decisions and often has the last word. So it takes a very strong and stable relationship to be able to re-define roles successfully, allowing the woman to start making the decisions, bringing home the wage packet instead of just pin money for holidays, and taking full responsibility for the children, without resentment showing on either side.

The wife may feel very sorry for her disabled husband, because she has seen an active life cut short in such a tragic way. But she may also begin to feel sorry for herself, and not surprisingly, because she has had to take on a lot more than she bargained for. The children may have realized the full horror of the situation at first, but eventually they will go back to making their normal demands and expect to have what they had before. The able-bodied partner in these circumstances may say very little for fear of hurting someone who has already suffered so much, both physically and emotionally; but in fact if these feelings can be put into words, and discussed in the context of mutual respect and love, then there is a greater chance of survival. It is in the supression of these feelings of anger and resentment that the danger lies.

In any crisis situation, the moral and practical help of friends and neighbours and colleagues can mean a great deal. For the couple facing sudden disablement the tremendous strains can be greatly alleviated with outside help. Without such co-operation many couples would not be able to survive. One woman who was suddenly struck with multiple sclerosis could not even go to the toilet by herself. Her husband moved house nearer his factory and made arrangements with his employer for his wife to be able to contact him by buzzer whenever she needed him. This is co-operation at an exceptional level. It was the difference between life and death for this woman.

This first chapter on marriage has put little emphasis on sex itself because it is after all only part of marriage, albeit an important part. However it is vital, before moving on to sexual relations, to stress that for some handicapped people sex without marriage may be all that they need or are capable of. Society is gradually accepting this solution for people in all walks of life. There is no longer a stigma attached to such a liaison, which is good news for those handicapped people for whom marriage can never be on the cards.

In the same way marriage without sex can be a viable proposition, and a satisfactory solution for many who would find sexual intercourse impossible physically or psychologically. But it is important for both of the partners in this kind of relationship to make sure that their feelings about sex are openly and frankly expressed. It is no good a couple getting married with one partner imagining that sex is going to be part of his or her life and the other thinking not. For a couple to be able to live in harmony together without sexual expression they must know in their own minds that this is a fact and that they have made the decision together—that there will be nothing further than petting and caressing and that they are happy with this formula. But neither should make the assumption that the other does not mind.

For the largest proportion of handicapped people, however, sex within marriage is the ideal, just as it is for most of society, despite our changing attitudes and morals. But it must be stressed that sex is only part of the total marriage relationship, and that if a couple are not satisfying each other's emotional needs then a wild sex life is not going to make up for it. By the same token an unsatisfactory sex life can put an enormous strain on other areas of the marriage.

4

Marriage (2)

We are living in a society today in which sexual acrobatics are considered quite normal and the Kama Sutra is supposed to be everybody's bedside reading. The fact that the majority of married couples in Britain still make love in the one 'missionary' position (i.e. the man on top of the woman), without any variation at all, is evidence that the heavy sexual propaganda of the last decade still has to make its big impact; but all this talk about sexual gymnastics, even if it is mostly hot air, can still leave the disabled person feeling even more under-privileged than he does anyway. This is particularly the case in a marriage between an able-bodied partner and someone disabled.

So straightaway let me reiterate that the aim of this book is not to make people feel dissatisfied with what they have got. Raising expectations too high may ruin their present satisfactions quite unnecessarily, so I am not trying to suggest that the disabled are missing something. What I am saying is that it is important always to be realistic. The disabled person has a real world like everyone else. If the reality of his world is that he can only lie back and let his wife make love to him, then there is no point in building up his fantasies about all the marvellous things they get up to in the sophisticated sex manual; but the disabled should not have to accept the general constraints put upon them by other people, such as their unsuitability to have sex and sexual feelings at all, or the inappropriateness of their marrying. They should explore their total situation and see how it can be improved and enriched—but always with realism.

Take for instance the woman of 45 who had had severe arthritis for many years and was unable to have intercourse with her husband without considerable pain. When she went into hospital for an operation for total hip replacement she found that the other patients often spoke of their own relations with their husbands. Some of them said quite honestly that, although their pain actually was severe, it was a good excuse for not having sex because they'd never got much out of it and they were only too pleased not to be 'bothered' very often. After her operation she was too shy to ask the doctor whether intercourse might damage her new hip, and as he didn't mention the subject she was very uncertain as to what she should do. Fortunately, when she got home, she was confident enough to discuss it with her husband, and, experimenting together, they gradually re-established a mutually satisfactory sex-life for themselves.

But many couples despair and give up because they are given so little help. Others unfairly blame their physical condition for their lack of sex feeling.

A man of 50 who went into hospital with a severe attack of bronchitis and pneumonia had some diminution of sexual desire before he was admitted. He felt like sex about once a week, but his wife was not over-enthusiastic. After his discharge he was tired and afraid of over-exciting himself, and as his wife made no demands it was two or three months before they had sex together again. After that it seemed to happen only once a month or even less, and he was quite certain that his illness was the cause of his increasing lack of libido.

The frequency of intercourse is very important especially for a man in his 40s or 50s or 60s. Men reach their sexual peak in late teens and early twenties, but thereafter sexual performance depends chiefly on feelings about sex and a partner's response; so if at 40 his wife is going off sex, then he is likely to lose interest too. After a spell in hospital, or any period when he does not perform, the sex urge may gradually disappear unless he makes a positive effort to resume; he may then quite wrongly blame his illness for this decreasing interest. There are many men who feel that after illnesses like heart attacks they should stop having sex. Most are reluctant to seek advice on the subject, and advice is rarely given spontaneously. Immediately after discharge from hospital sex might be too strenuous; but once a flight of stairs can be managed without difficulty, gentle sex is not going to overtax the heart. The frustration and worry of strong sexual feelings that can't be relieved, are likely to do more damage than normal release of tension. In these circumstances it might be advisable for a wife to masturbate her husband, or to have intercourse with her taking the more active superior position, so that her man has to undergo as little physical activity as possible.

Sex is in many ways as good as a tonic from the doctor for most people; it gives a feeling of well-being, and for men of manliness. And this boost is particularly valuable for those with a disablement. It is not only the physical pleasure of orgasm that's so important. Equally valuable is the pleasure that comes from giving pleasure, the psychic boost of being acknowledged as a lover and experiencing the satisfied response of a loved partner. This is a real basis of femininity and masculinity.

Psychological and emotional responses are an integral part of lovemaking. They awaken desire and influence performance, and it is these that need to be looked at if a couple are experiencing sex problems. Impotence and frigidity are nearly always caused by unacknowledged emotions. Jealousy, resentment, anger, insecurity and feelings of inferiority, both conscious and unconscious, can prevent and block the communication that should take place during intercourse. For sex is not just a physical act, it is a means of telling your partner your feelings, your love, and your joys; of sharing a deep unconscious pool of real individuality.

The saying that nothing succeeds like success applies very aptly to sex. The reverse—the fear of failure, the dread of not being able to achieve an erection—can be enough to prevent a man making it. His partner may be partially responsible if she has expressed or hinted at any feelings of doubt or scorn. He may wonder if his performance is going to match that of an able-bodied man. All these fears and anxieties can make him impotent even though there is no physical reason why he should not have an erection. We saw in the previous chapter how feelings of resentment and anger and inferiority can so easily arise in a couple who have to cope with serious disablement. Impotence or frigidity may be one of the first signs of this marital stress.

In all of these situations it may be helpful for a couple to seek outside advice from a third party. Unfortunately, counselling services for the disabled are still thin on the ground, and organizations dealing with marriage guidance and family planning are sometimes not geared to the specific problems of the disabled. Nevertheless, counselling can play a vital role in helping the handicapped come to terms with the sexual limitations imposed by their disability, and in helping them to understand the deeper psychological causes of their sexual difficulties. There are however, many physical reasons for sex problems in marriage; but here too, although each couple is different from any other, there are certain common areas of difficulty where general helpful advice can be given.

Background and convention are still probably the two most important influences in a couple's sex life. There is sometimes a cultural norm that anything other than sex in the dark, at night, under the covers, without a word being spoken, is dirty and sinful. Experimentation is a step down along the slippery slope to licentiousness and hell; if a hand or an arm is disabled or legs are stiff, that's just too bad—and you have to go without. Anyone brought up with these rigid attitudes is obviously going to have problems in adapting his feelings to match his limited physical capabilities; for the physical limitations bring emotional deprivation in their wake.

Hands or arms which have lost feeling and agility may have difficulty in caressing, stroking and subtly exciting the hair, skin and sensitive sexual nerve endings of the partner—and then also in registering that partner's response. It is very necessary, therefore, for anyone with these limitations to develop other tactile areas. Toes, feet, legs, tongue, teeth, lips, can all give and receive sensation; and many couples are gradually coming to accept that any 'pleasuring' of husband and wife together, as long as they are both happy about it, is good.

Oral sex, cunnilingus and fellatio, are beginning to be more widely practised and accepted. The taboos of earlier years are gradually disappearing, and the subject is being explored in books and films. It is certainly not suitable for every couple, but it may offer a new dimension of experience and mutual pleasure for many disabled, and help to make up for some of the other problems they are experiencing.

Many of the standards and taboos that are taken into marriage are the internalization of parents' standards, whether real or imagined; and couples are often released from their constrictions by the more permissive attitudes of those whom they identify as being in authority to them. So it is that a doctor, or a warden, or a counsellor can, by gentleness and understanding, 'give permission' for new experiences to be tested and tasted.

Stiffness and pain in the legs can make it difficult for husband or wife to enjoy sex, and some with severe arthritis of hips or knees, or spasticity of the lower limbs, find intercourse in the more usual position almost impossible to achieve. There is however a whole range of positions, where penetration takes place from the rear, husband behind wife. They can stand, kneel, sit or lie across each other and find a great variety of positions in which intercourse can be enjoyed. This obviously requires experimentation, and often practice and ingenuity, but most couples can eventually find some position that will give them comfort and satisfaction.

There are excellent books of photographs which most couples will find useful. It is unnecessary and probably greedy to hope to use them all, or even most of them, but they offer a range of suggestions which may be of help. There is always value in couples reading sex books together, for they encourage communication, by offering a framework of mutual experience, even if the experience is only visual. As a society, we tend not to speak of our real sexual feelings, and our sexual needs; we tend to be shy and often prudish about putting our thoughts and feelings into words. It may be inappropriate to communicate too fully with everyone, but within marriage a feedom to tell your partner what you like to do, or have done to you, nearly always increases the pleasure that both receive.

If for some reason it is unsuitable for the husband to over-exert himself, or if he finds difficulty in maintaining his balance in the superior position, a reversal of positions with the wife on top can give pleasure and satisfaction to both. The problems for those with spinal injury may be very great but can be partly overcome. Most men can manage to achieve erection within six months of their original injury, and some can experience and enjoy orgasm even though they have apparently no local sensation. Women, similarly, can have a loss of vaginal feeling; but they can still experience great comfort and satisfaction in intercourse, giving pleasure and discovering that they are still loved and lovable.

Unfortunately society apparently brings us up to believe

that sex should be intercourse or nothing. Mutual masturbation—the exciting manual stimulation of clitoris or penis—
is abhorrent to many; and women in particular often find
difficulty in allowing themselves to reach a climax, or helping
their husband, by this method. There is often at the back of
their minds a whole mythology about masturbation and
dirtiness. But touching is good and pleasurable, and every
couple should try to explore the erogenous zones that they
each enjoy—thighs, ears, breasts, abdomen, nipples, buttocks,
shoulders, each have their own particular feeling.

This is of course true for all couples, but it is particularly
important for those who have their range of experience
limited by disability. If pain is the main problem it might
help to take pain-relieving tablets before going to bed, to
prevent each session of lovemaking from being a session of
agony. It might also be worth considering wearing a brace or
collar or corset during intercourse, if this prevents pain.

Sex is a matter of habit, and it is a habit you can get out
of. Many couples, particularly if their disabilities are severe,
and the sex act is almost impossible to achieve spontaneously without a great deal of preparation, will find that it
plays a less important part in their lives as time goes by. This
is understandable. Nevertheless couples can still experience a
considerable amount of emotional comfort, simply by lying
side by side and enjoying the gentlest of caresses.

It is because physical closeness and the caring touch can
bring so much comfort and reassurance to a marriage that it
is most important to sleep in a double bed. I am against single
beds for almost any married couple, because I believe that
the psychological as well as physical gulf between two singles
is so great that it can eventually result in a couple drifting
apart themselves. Even for the able-bodied who sleep
separately, getting out of one bed and into another,
especially in winter in a cold bedroom, takes such an effort
of willpower that many people think twice before bothering.
And that is how the physical expression of love can begin to
disappear completely. How much more likely that the
disabled will abandon the initiative, if the effort to move
from one side of the room to the other is hazardous and even
painful. If you are already in bed together, even if sexual
intercourse is rare, you are still close and can communicate
simple feelings of love and tenderness just by touching an

arm or stroking a limb. It keeps a couple in touch with each other. And touching with no clothes on, even without sexual intercourse can be extremely comforting and pleasurable. Sex can disappear only too easily out of the life of a married couple if they turn their backs on each other too often.

If a disabled partner finds there are times when he or she suffers particularly from pain or discomfort, and is likely to disturb the other by a restless night, then obviously a move to a single bed is sensible. In that event it might be advisable to have two singles that zip together, or a double with a spare single somewhere else.

Throughout this chapter there has been an assumption that it is always possible for husband and wife to modify their needs to meet the other's limitations, whether these be physical or psychological. But some couples, even though they try very hard, may find it impossible to come to terms with the lack of sexuality that their disablement causes. Sex is a normal physical appetite; and occasionally a man or a woman may find it almost impossible to carry on normal social relationships with people at work if their sex tensions have not been relieved. Preaching self-restraint may be no answer for them; celibacy is not easy for everybody, and the work environment can place inordinate sexual strains on such people.

It may be appropriate for some of them to decide that, since the warmth, love and companionship of marriage are so important, and since marriage to their present partner means so much to them, then the missing sexual satisfaction should be found elsewhere. I am not suggesting that this is going to be a solution for everyone, for most couples still regard sexual experience outside marriage as 'unfaithfulness'. But standards and attitudes in this respect are changing, and there are couples nowadays who can tolerate some sharing of their partners, if this enables a secure loving relationship to continue between them. If unfaithfulness involves rejection of the marriage partner, then this will obviously be destructive; but if husband or wife can't provide the necessary sexual release, it may be 'right' for some couples to look elsewhere. Obviously this will only work if both husband and wife agree and if they both understand all the implications. But I believe that there are many badly disabled men and women who would not only tolerate the situation, but would be glad to know that their spouse was having essential needs met.

In the context of marriage for the handicapped, the question of whether or not to have children looms large. The instinctive reaction of many people is that the disabled should not have children. Yet I would shrink from saying anything so categorical, when I know from personal experience that there are thousands of children saddled with quite inadequate but so-called able-bodied parents! This judgment of society is just another way of saying that the handicapped are not quite adult, and that decisions have to be made for them. But who has the right to say who may reproduce and who may not? Obviously practical considerations have to be weighed up before any couple decide to raise a family. Many will see that their marriage and their finances would not be able to stand the extra burden of a child. Many husbands may recognize that their wives would just not be able to cope with a child. Small children for one thing need a great deal of attention. They need and deserve picking up and carrying, especially up to the age of two. A disabled mother may have to deprive her child of this form of communication and loving. It is possible of course to balance against this a later situation when the child can help to fetch and carry, as long as this does not make the child begin to feel the parents themselves are a burden.

Again, background, upbringing and personality play an important part. Take the case of the blind man in his twenties who married a sighted girl. He had no qualms about the possibility of producing a blind child, although it was a very remote chance. His own childhood, he said, had been so happy that he did not think blindness was so terrible a handicap. However the Spastics Society have reported that: 'Children of severely handicapped parents may have emotional problems which could lead to a need for counselling.' In a study of eighteen couples in which one or both of the parents were blind it was found that fifteen families had some difficulties. These could not however be blamed on blindness alone.

A spastic man, with normal speech but a clumsy walk, married to a non-handicapped wife, tells of the quite severe emotional problems this brought to their children. The son, from the time he started school, wanted to avoid being seen

40

with his father in public; in time he refused to bring his friends to the house, and the strained relationship between the two was not brought into the open or its problems solved until the son was virtually grown up. The daughter did badly at school, and suffered from migraine, although she was always affectionate to her father. Again it was not until adolescence that he discovered how hard she had been fighting for him against girls at school over the years, and what a deep emotional effect her loyalty to him in keeping quiet about it had had on her.

Children of blind parents have to take on particular responsibilities because in some ways they become parents to their parents, watching across roads, guarding them from obstacles in the home. From an early age they have to accept adult roles, and in some ways miss out on the experience of wholly dependent childhood. The danger of this is that when they themselves bring up a family they will expect their own children to do things for them.

Clearly considerations like the extent of the disability, and the husband's earning capacity, as well as the personality of the parents, must weigh heavily in coming to a decision about having a family. But the decision must be the couple's, not society's.

A particular pitfall is if the disabled couple have a child as an affirmation to the world of their masculinity and femininity, and not because they want a child for himself. This is where counselling can be of value in helping them to examine their unconscious motives rationally and realistically. The importance of genetic counselling in hereditary diseases is obvious and there are centres up and down the country where couples can go and discuss this aspect of their marriage and have tests. I go into this in more detail in Chapter 10.

Any decision about family planning must naturally lead on to the choice of a contraceptive, and it is of paramount importance that the method used should be acceptable to both partners. There is plenty of literature available to help in making a choice, and the Family Planning Association will provide information by post. People are, even today, a little diffident about asking for contraceptive advice, and many disabled couples retain at the back of their minds the feeling that they should not be having sex at all.

Two young spastics who married in their early twenties told me how they had gone into marriage with very little knowledge of the facts of life. No one had spoken to them about sex; they had just picked up scraps of information as they went along, being reassured that they need not worry about such things because they would not be having any anyway! In their turn therefore they felt reluctant to ask for advice.

A lack of sex education in the past (see Chapter 8) may have planted all sorts of curious notions in the mind which influence thinking on contraception. Prime among these is the guilt attached to sex, which sometimes prevents people actually buying or acquiring contraceptives in advance, because they are unwilling to admit to themselves that they have sex on the mind. Many a girl has become pregnant for this very reason. For the disabled there are also the problems of access to chemists' shops in high-street complexes, or barbers shops and 'gents' which are often in basement premises. All these physical obstacles need to be overcome, but counselling and open discussion at an early stage can help to break down the barriers of fear and shame and ignorance.

The choice of contraceptive must be left to the individual couple, but choice can only be effectively made when all the options are known. Only too often a couple is persuaded to use a particular method, because it is 'good' or 'reliable' or because the doctor or counsellor uses it himself, without taking into account the prejudices or hang-ups or fears of that particular pair. Attitudes are often determined by old wives' tales, or stories of what happened to a friend of a friend; and experience has shown that the safest contraceptive is only safe if that couple feels secure and happy in its use. Many couples use coitus interruptus (or withdrawal) because they have found no other way; and this is notoriously unsafe, as well as being emotionally thwarting for any couple, but particularly for those who have not got the physical agility to withdraw at exactly the right time. The safe period, another method which requires no medical help, is also contraceptively unsafe, as well as preventing spontaneity in sex.

The sheath, which is one of the most widely used methods of contraception, requires an element of physical agility on the part of the man. He has to reach to a side table to take hold of it, fit it with a certain amount of dexterity at the right moment, take care not to tear it and then remove it later—simple enough for the dextrous, whose arms and hands obey them, but quite tricky for the disabled. When it is used efficiently it is very safe and has the additional advantage of preventing the transmission of venereal disease.

The Dutch Cap used in conjunction with chemical creams is effective; but a handicapped wife may find difficulty in placing it in position if she has not free use of her hands or an ability to bend her hips. However, it could be a good method for the able-bodied woman with a disabled husband, because she can then take all the responsibility for contraception off his shoulders. It is a simple method for women to use, especially if they are accustomed to internal sanitary protection. It also avoids some of the anxiety which may be associated with other methods.

There are undoubtedly certain groups of woman for whom the contraceptive pill (hormonal contraception) is unsuitable, although its use is becoming more and more widespread and it is contraceptively one of the safest methods. These groups of women include those with previous history of blood clotting and blood disease, and those who suffer from migraine or varicose veins or who have had previous liver damage. The pill sometimes causes depression and transient symptoms like headaches, and some brands cause a severe weight gain which may be a serious and unnecessary problem to somebody who is already physically disabled. Some of the symptoms disappear with time or can be alleviated by a change of pill. An extra bonus for the many women who take the pill (and the number runs into millions in Britain today) is that there is often a reduction in menstrual flow, which could be a godsend to any woman who spends a lot of time in a wheelchair or holds down a job where a trip to the loo means a long walk.

Finally there is the I.U.D. (intra uterine device), commonly known as the coil, which needs to be fitted by a doctor and then requires no other particular preparation for intercourse. There are however two small disadvantages. It has a tendency to cause heavier periods, which, as we have seen, can be very inconvenient for the woman in a wheelchair; and sometimes it causes bouts of tummy cramps.

Whichever method is chosen, however, the main point

about contraception is that it should be as effective as possible, because few couples can afford mistakes. Contraception can be almost 100% safe, so it is foolish not to take advantage of the freedom that these advances offer. If there is a failure of contraception, termination of pregnancy would probably not be refused to a handicapped woman. Nevertheless an abortion is an experience most women would prefer to avoid. The disabled woman who has settled for remaining childless may find it very difficult, perhaps impossible, to say yes to an abortion once she finds that she is pregnant. She may have made a rational decision not to have children, but deep down in her heart she may feel very torn if she has to make a decision because a mistake has been made. A lot of so-called mistakes arise from a sub-conscious need to become pregnant; and some women, once accidental pregnancy is determined, realize consciously how much they wanted the baby. So although the abortion brings relief, it can also bring grief to many.

It may be easier for a couple to discuss contraception together if they can see it not so much as a way of stopping children as a way of achieving a happy life together without burdening their handicap any more. They can then enjoy sex for what it is, and enjoy the relationship with each other without being afraid of bringing children into the world.

Other solutions include sterilization and vasectomy; but they are not operations that people undertake lightly. There is still considerable opposition among the medical profession to sterilization of women, although the situation of a disabled woman may be viewed sympathetically. Vasectomy is easier to obtain, but many men resent or are afraid of the operation, although it is a very simple procedure without any after-effects on sex feelings.

Any discussion of childbirth and family planning must embrace the subject of artificial insemination. While it is still a difficult principle for many people to accept without repugnance, nevertheless under certain circumstances—if, for instance, the husband cannot manage intercourse but can ejaculate—it could provide the disabled with the one solution to their family problem. For such a couple, A.I.H. (artificial insemination by husband) might be a possibility. A.I.D. (artificial insemination by donor) is rarely practised in this country because it takes a very mature couple to cope with the psychological problems that may arise. However there are a few doctors who might be prepared to help. There is always, unfortunately, the knowledge that the child is the mother's not the father's, and the husband can then feel shut off from the relationship between a mother and child.

The sex problems of the handicapped are very much those of everybody else. And just as there are no clear cut answers for the able-bodied there are none for the disabled. Everyone has to solve his own. However bringing them into the open, acknowledging that they exist, putting them into perspective, must help anyone to be a real person in the real world, instead of being left as a hot-house plant without feelings.

5

Parents

The arrival of every new born child into the family is an event of considerable importance, attended by excited and happy ritual. Cartoons and reality alike have nervous fathers smoking their lungs to a standstill surrounded by a heap of cigarette ends. Whether the child is the firstborn or the fourteenth it is rarely received without some rejoicing, bunches of flowers and congratulatory telegrams, heralding a great achievement on the part of both parents as though this were the first infant ever brought into the world. Each delivery is a small miracle, and even in circumstances where the child was unplanned or really unwanted these feelings are cast aside to give the new arrival the welcome it deserves. For nine months the growing foetus has been a real person in the eyes of the parents: a boy with blue eyes, a girl with fair hair, it has an identity for them from the day it was conceived, and names are bandied about even though its sex is unknown. There may be a preference for a boy or a girl, but the disappointment of it being the 'wrong' sex is shortlived.

However, few parents have not given at least a fleeting thought to the prospect of their next child being born less than perfect. They know it happens to the most unlikely people. It could happen to them.

The shock that strikes with the news that the new arrival does not come up to expectations, is in some way malformed or abnormal, is so total that few mothers, or fathers for that matter, ever really recover. The sense of failure is over-whelming. The mind and the memory search for a clue, some explanation, for some meaning. Different interpretations and heart-searching go on. Was it an Act of God, a punishment? Perhaps I should have eaten more vitamins/taken iron tablets/rested more. Maybe a long forgotten ancestor can be blamed. Or a childhood illness. Unfortunately, explanations

46

are as yet still hard to come by, and with nothing concrete to blame, parents blame themselves. They live with this sense of guilt and failure rarely assuaged.

Today the organizations formed to group together particular disabilities do go a long way to support both parents and the disabled child, morally, physically and economically. Government measures are gradually improving their lot and their opportunities. But the fact remains that a large majority of parents face a lonely lifetime of caring for the handicapped child. Some do decide in the child's interest (or their own) that he should be put into a home where skilled care can give the child the chances it would never have at home. Obviously a decision like this depends on the extent of the child's disability, on the personality and economic circumstances of the parents, and on whether or not there are other, demanding, children in the family.

By and large it is accepted, although still open to debate, that, for most disabled children, to be put into a home, 'to be put away' in the old sense, is psychologically damaging and can never replace the home environment. However enlightened the residential care, there is nearly always some feeling of rejection on the part of the child and of failure for the parents. Yet there are three questions which need scrupulous examination before this option is dismissed: how well the parents cope and whether their marriage is under strain, whether the other children in the family are suffering, and whether the handicapped child would positively benefit from residential care in the way of opportunities for training, for meeting more friends and for generally having more fun and a fuller life.

It is sometimes said that the family with a handicapped child is a handicapped family, and that tremendous strain is put upon each individual. For instance, the family with a badly crippled child is prevented from doing together all the things normal families take for granted. They may not be able to manage traditional family holidays by the seaside, or at least not enjoy them to the full, with the problems of getting wheelchairs up hotel steps and through restaurant doors, and of a mother or sister always remaining behind to care for the disabled one or to keep him company while the others explore cliff-top walks. Many families, of course, accept these restrictions stoically and devise a pattern of life which reduces these limitations to a minimum. Some say that a handicapped child has brought the family closer together and instilled in the other children a capacity for caring that might otherwise have remained dormant. But these are potentially explosive situations. The other children may resent the extra care and attention and even money lavished on the disabled brother and sister, especially if financial sacrifices have to be made. They may want to go out and play in the street when the mother asks them to stay in and be with the less able child. The other children may, with or without justification, begin to think that the household revolves around that one child.

One of the dangers all along is that the handicapped child will be over-protected, over-cossetted and treated more like an endearing pet than a human being. Such a child will then face the problems that I have described in the chapter on adolescence, where he or she is shielded from life's slings and arrows and grows into a hot-house plant, a two-dimensional being, unbruised and untouched by unpleasant everyday experiences.

Some parents realize that they have got to allow their handicapped child to take risks, to cross the road unaided, to be independent, because if the child is not allowed to take risks the parents are risking something far worse than a potential road accident. A blind man I know leads a professional life that involves a great deal of travel on trains and buses; when I told him how much I admired his courage, he shrugged his shoulders and said that he had gained his self-confidence as a child. His parents had allowed him to go out with lots of other kids, and he had learned quite early on how much strangers are willing to help the disabled get about. He was not in the least afraid of asking for help, and this way he travelled regularly across London by day and night.

The influence of parents on their children is vital. For the handicapped child it is not only vital but decisive. No parent is perfect when it comes to bringing up children. We can read all the child psychology books ever written and still make colossal mistakes. It has nothing to do with how well we are educated or whether we come from poor homes or privileged backgrounds. Any glance at a daily newspaper demonstrates that debutantes and heirs to fortunes are as likely to turn out

48

social misfits as a child reared on a street corner. As every Spock proselyte knows, it is not the *quantity* of love a child receives in its formative years, but the *quality* of that love that counts. A parent who stonewalls a child's natural rebelliousness, who ties the apron strings in a tight knot and tries to deny that he will one day get up and leave, probably without asking, is heading for bitter unhappiness. It is achieving the balance between protection and freedom that most parents find so difficult and frustrating.

To a greater or lesser extent most parents, even when they are old and grey, will always see their children in gym slips and short pants. This is perfectly natural. The mother of the 40-year-old son will always worry that he is not getting enough to eat. The father of a mother of three will keep advising her to drive carefully. It is normal parental concern, an expression of love, which does not end with the age of majority.

For the parents of a handicapped child the situation is the same but magnified many times. If they feel guilty at having produced an imperfect human being, the tendency is to compensate by being super-parents. They make heroic sacrifices to give the child the best, and shelter him from pain as well as pleasure, unable to see that pain can be productive; but by making martyrs of themselves they make the child more helpless than he need be. If they know that they are going to have to provide for their child's basic needs—three meals a day, a roof over his head, bathing and dressing—all his life, it is easiest to cope if they think of him as a perpetual child, a child they can control. An emergent adult, an adolescent, is more difficult because the whole process of growing up involves the making of decisions for yourself. If you have never been allowed or encouraged to make decisions then obviously you do not acquire the skill. This skill may be no more involved than choosing a dress for a party; weighing up parents' advice against your own desires when it comes to choosing between fashionable shoes and sensible brogues; deciding which cinema to go to, which girl to ring up, whether to go camping or to a football match; or whether to stay in and do homework or meet a friend and do it hurriedly in the morning—but these are all the fundamental ways we have to make decisions as we grow up and learn to relate to others and act responsibly.

49

The handicapped child who has these decisions made for him, or does not have the chance to face the situations that produce them, is doubly handicapped. He will find it difficult to behave like an adult when the time comes. Not surprising, then, that people involved with the handicapped sometimes complain about their immature behaviour and inability to fit in socially. Yet they may be the ones who are preventing the child becoming an adult person, and behaving like an adult, by denying him the responsibilities that create adult attitudes. The dilemma for parents is that, because their days are more or less ruled by the routine imposed by the child's handicap, it is easier to say 'We will lunch at 12 and have fish' and 'You will wear that blue dress today' because it fits in with the smooth running of the household. When you have a disabled child you have to be highly organized in order to cope; but if you want people to behave responsibly you have to allow them to make decisions for themselves and take risks.

If they do not get the chance to choose the clothes they wear, what time they have tea and what they eat for supper, they may well be unable to make the more vital choices later on. It is very nice to have things done for you—but not all the time. If a child takes an hour to dress himself in the morning, surely it is better that he get up early to do it for himself rather than sleep in an extra hour and be dressed by his mother in ten minutes? This is independence and personal achievement and it builds self-respect. Dependence is one of the reasons that handicapped children often see themselves as an extension of their parents without an identity of their own. Yet it is important, even more so than for the ordinary able-bodied child, that the handicapped child has this identity. Part of growing up is beginning to know who you are and that you exist as a person in your own right.

A lot of children, handicapped and able-bodied, feel that the person they are presenting to the world is not the real them, and that the person the world wants to see is not really them either. They know that there is a very different person inside simply trapped there by circumstances, by the expectations and demands of their parents, and also by their own fear of giving themselves away—fear for instance, that if they show their real selves the world will not be too impressed and people will stop liking them. Most children grow easily out of these fantasies. For the handicapped child the situation is aggravated by the knowledge that he has to be looked after and must therefore be ready with a smile of gratitude and always be nice because people are always nice to him. But in fact often he is not grateful. After all why should he be? It is not his fault he came into the world as he is. However, he has the fear that if he expresses his ingratitude his parents and others may reject him. So he is as nice as possible so that the loving and the caring continue.

This may seem a harsh diagnosis for both the handicapped child and his parents to swallow; but given close, open-minded examination, it goes a long way to rationalizing the inner fears of the handicapped child as he fights his anger at being less than whole. He knows it would be cruel to his parents to be anything but thankful, but at the same time he is bursting with pent-up feelings of anger and frustration. This mixture of power and impotence, the capacity, on the one hand, to rule parents' lives and to hurt, and the knowledge, on the other, that he is dependent on them and really at their mercy, both emotionally and physically, gives the handicapped child terrible feelings of ambivalence. He does not really know where he stands.

The crisis of identity goes further and extends to the child's sexuality. Parents of today's younger generation still have difficulty acknowledging them as potentially sexual beings, capable of loving and being loved and of mating and rearing a family. To acknowledge this means accepting that the child is growing up and will soon be an adult. How parents cope with this depends in the first place on their own attitudes towards sex, how they themselves were brought up, the kind of relationships they have experienced and the quality of their own marriage; and in the second on whether they will have any life of their own when the child has said his goodbyes, or whether there will be an empty void in their lives with nothing to take his place.

Accepting the sexuality of a disabled child is even more difficult and embarrassing, and the common reaction, as we have said already, is to ignore the subject in the hope that it will go away. Again this is part of the Peter Pan syndrome: keep the child child-like and the question of sex will not arise. Unfortunately, normal, healthy, sexual urges have a nasty habit of getting the better of ignorance and neglect.

51

For one thing there is only a small proportion of handicapped adolescents who are so disabled that they could not have sex. I am not advocating promiscuity, but I believe that a large number of teenagers who are disabled will want to experiment with sex just as normal kids do. So parents have a duty to encourage relationships and friendships with the opposite sex, giving their children sex education and teaching them its implications.

The problem is that parents see no future for their handicapped children in the marriage stakes; and as sex and marriage are still as inseparable in most people's minds as the proverbial horse and carriage, there seems no point to them in bringing it up at all.

Yet the handicapped live in a real world like the rest of us, and sexuality is part of that real world. It is not just a question of church bells and intercourse. Sexuality is a form of communication, the way we relate to other people, to the opposite sex, our own children and our elders. It is an expression of love and a way of behaving as a human being; and if the handicapped child is denied this sexuality, he is going to find it difficult to get on with others. It is essential, for instance, for each of us to have a sexual identity, to see ourselves as masculine or feminine. Most children learn to do this in relation first of all with their parents. Partially they identify with the parent of their own sex and partially they relate to the one of the opposite sex, flirting and testing out feelings about what it is like to be a boy or a girl; and depending on the reaction of the parents, they begin to taste what being a man or a woman is all about. The little boy is encouraged to look after his mother, and to protect her. The little girl stays at home and makes her daddy tea. This may sound old-fashioned in these days of Women's Lib, when the traditional roles are being challenged and boys are expected to wash up and girls to mend plugs. But what we are discussing is not a question of tasks but a question of identity in relation to other people and to the opposite sex.

The great danger is that the disabled child may be denied these opportunities to see himself as masculine or feminine, not only because the situations may not arise to 'protect Mummy' or 'help Daddy' (especially if the handicap is so great it would be ludicrous to suggest it in the first place), but also because, as I have already said, with parents foreseeing a sexless future, they do not want to do anything that will underline the child's inability to fulfil his or her role as a man or a woman.

However, times and attitudes are changing. In the future more handicapped people will marry, so parents have got to be more positive in bringing up their disabled children with this kind of future in view.

I know there are many valid fears in the hearts of parents when the subject of marriage and their handicapped children is aired. There is the fear for instance that a daughter may want to marry someone who appears not to be able to provide the care and attention that the parents have lavished so selflessly all those years. You could call this the apple-pie syndrome. How many girls strive for years to perfect their apple pies to meet the standards of their husband's mother's apple pies? It is of course quite likely that another handicapped person will never be able to offer the same standards of care. But does this necessarily rule out their chances of a happy marriage, fraught though it may be with domestic crises like making beds and mending roofs? A badly handicapped spastic who defied his handicap and achieved a university degree and then announced he was going to marry a handicapped girl, faced strong opposition from his parents. They felt he was doubling his problem not halving it. Having attempted unsuccessfully to shield him from the hazards of life they, in his own words, 'were almost responsible for ruining my life'. But he emphasized that they did it out of kindness. They thought they were doing their best for him.

There is also the fear of exploitation, the fear that a disabled son or daughter will fall too easily in love with someone who has shown them the slightest kindness, misinterpreting this kindness for something much deeper and hanging on to it like a straw in the wind. A girl in her late teens with muscular dystrophy was attending a day centre when she fell in love with one of the volunteer workers there. He promised to marry her, she got pregnant and he fled. The girl never knew whether in fact he would have married her later had she not conceived, and went home to her parents to have the baby. They are helping her cope, but life is very difficult for them. However, had her parents had the self-confidence to talk to her and tell her there was nothing wrong with sexual experience but that she should be careful not to get pregnant, giving her the necessary contraceptive advice, she might have benefited from the affair instead of having to ask her parents to pick up the pieces.

I know it is asking a great deal of parents to talk to their adolescent offspring about contraception. But parents of the handicapped will have to do this, just as parents of the able-bodied are gradually beginning to accept their responsibilities in this direction. And it is even more important for the former, because the handicapped often have not the mobility or the wide circle of friends that could help them get hold of the relevant information for themselves.

If the parents cannot themselves imagine how someone disabled could possibly appear attractive to an outsider, they may feel that anyone who shows interest must be doing so for some unhealthy reason. But this is not necessarily so. A couple with a spastic daughter who convinced themselves that she would never find a marriage partner were appalled when at 18 she fell in love with a boy she met at night school. She was not very badly handicapped, but they felt her chances were bleak; and they were so certain that the boy could not be serious, and so keen to protect her from getting hurt, that they told her an untruth about him, and pressed her to end the friendship. They were in their own fumbling way trying to save her from pain. Yet the girl might have learned much from the affair, and the chance of getting hurt would not have been any worse than for any other teenager.

Parents can always produce plenty of sound, practical reasons why a marriage they oppose is out of the question, without actually voicing their opinion of the unsuitability of the partner. This applies whether the partner is handicapped or not; but if the partner is handicapped there is probably more reason to question motivation. Some people do marry through pity for their partner, and such a motivation is questionable simply because pity does not always last a lifetime; it can turn to resentment and produce a great deal of unhappiness. If the initial emotions of pity and dependence can develop into something on a more equal footing— mutual respect through self knowledge and shared experience—then such a marriage can be a great success; but it is dangerous territory.

The question we must keep asking is to what extent parents and others can actually stop a marriage they disapprove of when both parties are past the age of majority and certainly of consent. The non-handicapped are quite free to defy parents' wishes as long as they comply with the law of the land. Many do—for better or for worse. They have the mobility and economic independence to do it. They probably have the emotional independence too, having unknotted the apron strings long ago. If they make a mess of the marriage there are always alternatives other than running home to mother. The handicapped girl or boy who makes an unsuccessful marriage may be forced to eat humble pie and return home—but this is no reason to stop them taking chances in the first place.

Parents have to ask themselves with piercing honesty why they are opposing such a relationship. Is it because they do not want to be usurped? Would they then be facing empty lives? Do they dread the arrival of grandchildren, with the sinking feeling that if anything goes wrong they will be lumbered? Is the very thought of two handicapped people making love rather distasteful to them?

These intrusions into the hearts and minds of parents may sound cold and cruel, but they are voiced to help parents understand their innermost feelings and to cope with the possibility of their children loving someone else. Obviously they want the best for their children—most parents do. But to give a handicapped child all the creature comforts yet to deny him the chance to love and be loved (and maybe to get hurt on the way) is to inflict a punishment equal to the disability itself.

There are no clear-cut solutions. The Department of Health and Social Security, in a study of the 'Care of the child with spina bifida', admitted that few parents receive the 'continuing care they so clearly need'. This means support not just from social workers and medical staffs but from society itself. And that does not merely mean handouts at Christmas in response to pathetic appeals on radio and TV: these sometimes do more harm than good in segregating the handicapped from the rest of the population.

What is needed above all is moral support from the child's contemporaries and from neighbours, from—for want of a better phrase—the man in the street. This is nothing that legislation can bring about; only a metamorphic change in attitudes. A woman with a young spastic son told me how she took him in a push chair to the school coach pick-up point every morning, stopping on the way to shop or buy sweets. She felt that her neighbours avoided her; people in shops were suddenly preoccupied with their purchases and would do anything rather than look towards the pram and the boy. 'I just felt them thinking what a terrible thing it was to have a handicapped child. It was as though they were blaming me. This makes me feel even more embarrassed and ashamed and I shrink further and further away from social contacts. I know this is no good for Simon.'

There are some people who feel certain that, like those seasonal broadcast appeals, special schools only accentuate the feelings of the handicapped that they are 'different' from the rest of society. So integrate the handicapped into ordinary schools wherever possible, and society will begin to accept them as normal human beings and not objects of pity that an annual donation can expurgate from view.

It is argued by some on the other hand that one disabled child in a school of fit and healthy youngsters makes the disabled one feel even more different because he cannot run up stairs and lark around like the others. But on balance those few State and private schools that have accepted handicapped children say that among other things it gives the healthy ones a chance to learn that there are other, weaker members of the community who have to be considered. In one such school the boys were primed beforehand to accept a new disabled pupil as a challenge, as part of their community service. This same child had been attending a special school quite a way from his home and consequently had few friends in his neighbourhood until he began at the new school nearer home. His mother felt that even when his friends had left home to work or to marry at least her son knew all the families, and no one locally was any longer shy or embarrassed talking to him. He was part of the community instead of being a bit of a curiosity as he had been before. 'One thing that the ordinary school taught him was to be open about his disability, tell the other boys what it was like to be crippled, and what limitations it put upon him. The school were marvellous at encouraging him to do well the things he liked doing rather than striving for academic achievement.'

Children with handicapped brothers and sisters grow up to accept disability. But children with no experience of people

56

with scarred bodies and distorted limbs will stare with in-nocent curiosity and often naive amusement when they come into contact with a handicapped person. The latter is put on his guard and shrinks into a shell and the able-bodied kid learns nothing. But if they can meet day by day they will surely learn to see beyond the disability to the real person. The benefits of mixing are even greater for the handicapped child, who can begin to experience many of the normal growing-up processes he misses in a sheltered environ-ment. He can learn how to get on with people, stand up for himself, gain a measure of emotional independence. A more caring society must result.

Parents of the handicapped should remember that all adolescents have problems; many of the problems their child may be experiencing are probably similar to those of every ordinary child. The only way to help is to encourage the child to have as many outside contacts as possible and try not to bottle up frustrations. The handicapped child has also got to appreciate that he is not the only one with a problem. He must be helped to understand that the world is not full of normal people—and him. There are very few—particularly among the young—who are totally self-assured. In fact most of us are in some way disabled, either physically, mentally or psychologically. The girl with the spotty face, the short-sighted boy, the child with a strawberry mark, the fat and the skinny—they all think their problem is enormous, and they become scarred to a greater or lesser degree by it. How they cope though depends on their contacts with other people, their ability to relate.

Parents do derive great strength from other parents, and it is vital that they belong to on-going groups for discussion and for sharing experiences. At some stage every parent's child must cross the road or come in late. That day may be dreaded; but, if you can draw strength from the fact that other parents are going through the same torments and fantasies about the child being run over or seduced, then you may worry a little less.

The mother of a nine-year-old boy with spina bifida told me that a day never went by when she did not worry about her son's future. He was attending a special school and was in fact leading a comparatively independent life, but her fears seemed to overshadow everything he did. She went to see the headmaster for advice and he suggested she start a discussion group among parents, with the children's future as its main objective. This not only gave her a new interest but made her realize that her fears were shared with the other mothers and fathers. In a way she also began to feel that the future was not so bleak.

Parents of the able-bodied get as much advice as they can cope with these days on how to bring up their children. Magazines, newspapers and shelves of library books are constantly advising and educating. For the parents of the disabled, on the other hand, information and support is scarce. Yet they need it much more. There is, for example, a tremendous need for parents and others to give more practical encouragement to those handicapped adolescents capable of earning a living of their own. And this does not mean packing combs and threading beads. There is a huge section of higher-intellect disabled who could with the right backing be doing much more significant work than they are doing at present. A trade or profession of their own, with its financial as well as social rewards, can provide some of those opportunities for emotional and physical independence that the handicapped so crave and need.

The education of parents is even more vital when it comes to an understanding of the nature of their child's sexuality, because they have first to overcome their own inhibitions and eradicate many of their own prejudices before they can see their child's problem clearly.

Twenty years ago it was considered shocking for parents to be seen undressed by their children. Nowadays the majority of parents I meet accept this as normal behaviour; they bath quite happily with the children coming in and out of the bathroom, and undress without embarrassment. This helps the youngster to accept his body without shame. This kind of approach can be particularly useful for the handicapped child who may not have the same opportunities of feeling and touching his friends' bodies as normal children do in playgrounds and behind bushes. An extension of this experience is to give the handicapped child the opportunity to touch his parents' bodies, to lie close together in bed and know what it is like to be touched and experience the reciprocal feelings of warmth and trust. For some parents this may be difficult or almost impossible, because of their feelings of guilt about their bodies. Again, talking with other parents can help put these anxieties into perspective.

I have put considerable emphasis in this book on the subject of masturbation, because it is one of the last remaining taboos of Western civilization. People still do not talk about it easily. Many are still guilt-ridden about it. But it should figure in parents' teaching of handicapped children, because with less emotive attitudes it can help the handicapped to get the physical release they may otherwise be denied. Many parents find it an embarrassing and fraught subject, and some view it with disgust and abhorrence; but with open discussion, perhaps more reading on the subject, they might be able to see that masturbation is not 'dirty' and that it is just part of growing up. Some parents may want to help their handicapped children to masturbate where hands are limited in their movements. Others may be quite confident their children can cope alone. The aim either way should be to get rid of the connotations of guilt with which most of today's older generation view it. For one thing, the child who feels guilty about masturbating is likely to masturbate more rather than less. So he needs to have the opportunity to learn that it is normal adolescent behaviour which doesn't make you go blind and doesn't damage the health.

The disabled youngster is often a confused person. He does not get the support or lead from his contemporaries that most children do. His parents may be more reactionary in their views than the parents of the able-bodied, who are forced to change and are often influenced by the fresh air their own children bring into their lives. So his bewilderment about such preoccupying subjects as girl-friends, masturbation and his latent sexual feelings is often met with embarrassment and equal uncertainty. The answer lies in creating the sort of atmosphere at home in which the child feels confident enough to talk about his fears and frustrations, about the future and about marriage, knowing he will not be rebuffed by red-faced parents unable to cope with such dreaded subjects.

6

Residential care - staff problems

The question of change within residential homes for the physically and mentally handicapped, change involving more enlightened attitudes towards sex and the expression of sexuality, towards personal relationships and even the availability and acceptance of contraception, is something which burdens a great number of people today. It is a subject wrapped one minute in embarrassed verbiage and another in heated controversy. We all have our sexual hang-ups and inhibitions, and very few of us can discuss sex without these personal feelings getting in the way. So when we come to examine the situation in residential care units, and want to propose greater freedom of sexual expression for the disabled, we have to remember the circumstances under which these units were founded, which make it difficult now to bring about change without a conflict of moral values and a clash of interests.

Many of the homes and institutions in existence today were established maybe forty years ago in large country mansions surrounded by rural calm and remote from the realities of urban industrial life, and many of them have developed very much along the lines laid down by the founders. They were built on the love and care of dedicated staff, who moulded them according to their own principles of Christian morality, providing as good a life as possible for their charges, with poor financial reward and little in the way of independent lives for themselves. These people often had nursing backgrounds and worked with barely any direction from the people who originally set up the homes. It is difficult to find words to express society's debt to them, or to give them sufficient praise. Yet today they are still the

Cinderellas of the social services, over-worked, underpaid and very often under-qualified.

At another level, taking public responsibility for these homes and their running, are the management committees representing the sponsorship of the homes, be it local authority, church-based charity or the national organization representing a particular disability. By their very nature they may be comprised of people with very high moral and religious values, attracted to the work by the best motives of service and concern, and giving their time selflessly and without remuneration.

The homes today are running smoothly and happily along these lines. To many people, therefore, there seems no reason to change, to disturb the status quo, to burden the disabled with new worries and the already over-stretched staff with extra problems and probably extra work and responsibility.

Management committees and staff alike who may recognize that the time has come to rethink the values and attitudes of the past have nevertheless a pretty good idea of what might follow a policy of allowing residents greater freedom to develop personal relationships and explore their sexuality. They may want the handicapped in their care to get more out of life and enjoy the happiness that love and sex can bring. But these people have been put in their charge by parents who tend to make superhuman demands and expect the highest standards of behaviour. They know that it only takes one sniff of scandal, the merest suggestion that anything untoward is going on in the establishment under their control, however exaggerated or wrongly interpreted— not only does society frown, but funds have a nasty habit of drying up. After an article appeared in a responsible Sunday newspaper on the subject of the sexual rights of the handicapped, the warden of a very well known home for the physically disabled rang me up to say that he was worried it might affect the outcome of an appeal he was about to launch, and on which he depended for much-needed repairs and expansion.

If you are responsible for an establishment you want to keep it within the limits you know you can cope with. You want to run it efficiently. But this inevitably begs the question 'efficiently for whom?' The staff or the residents, the management committee or the donors? If you are giving charity to someone does this mean you have the right to expect them to conform to your standards and behave in the same way that you behave?

These questions are being asked increasingly in residential homes and hostels up and down the country. Not only because society is more aware of the rights of the individual and is discussing these rights openly, but also because the handicapped themselves are asking for certain rights. They are no longer cut off from the outside world. Radio and television bring them into daily contact with the spirit of the times we live in. Many of the professional people working with them have the chance to lead independent lives and have more modern values and standards. So both staff and residents are finding themselves at odds with others in control of residential homes who are trying to hold on to standards and moral principles which were more applicable twenty-five years ago, and who rarely ask themselves if change might be appropriate.

This is not to say that these standards and values are wrong. After all these staffs came to their jobs through the highest Christian motives. What is in question is the willingness of the disabled themselves to accept charity and care ungrudgingly, submissively. They are beginning to ask for a say in the running of their lives, for involvement in decisions that affect them. And above all they are questioning the moral values imposed upon them.

Many disabled people in residential care say that they are not treated as equals, as full human beings, and that they are rarely given the opportunity to behave like adults. The dilemma for staff is that very often residents have to be treated like children simply because they behave like children, without concern for others. And it is difficult to treat like adults those you have to care for completely, those who are totally dependent on you for all their simplest needs. So it may be a great temptation to hold on to the old authoritarian principles of care; and titles like housemother and matron do not help to dispel the old structured hierarchy, more in keeping with a public school than a permanent home.

There is no doubt that society is beginning to rethink its whole attitude to disablement and the sexual rights of the handicapped. But if we are to seek changes then we have to look carefully at what will happen if change takes place. Is it going to be possible to establish new conditions that may be so alien to the nature of some staff that they feel all their past efforts are for nought? Are they going to feel threatened by the idea of the disabled being allowed to be treated like adults, as equals rather than children—because in a sense this may mean they are losing control? After all, they may have worked in a residential unit for many years; their ideas may have stood the test of time, even though they appear old fashioned today; and when they themselves have perhaps remained unmarried and without any sex life, denying themselves the chance of personal fulfilment in order to serve the disabled, they are going to be a little disturbed by talk of the need for the disabled to enjoy sexual expression.

Over the years they have had drummed into them the importance of the institution's public reputation, because of their reliance on voluntary contributions and public funds. They have set themselves high moral standards to justify their unstinting devotion. So it is vital that their feelings, their values, their sacrifice, be considered. However, today no one can afford to ignore the fact that times are changing; that many of the old values and disciplines are being turned upside down. This applies to every institution, every society, every family unit. Fifty years ago I might have employed a staff of six to run my home, scrub floors, cook meals and so on. Today I'm lucky if I can find a daily help who might come in to clean as a favour. My attitude towards her is quite different from what it would have been a generation ago. I no longer tell her what to do, I ask her; and if she agrees then we are both satisfied. But today we are equals, not master and servant.

So those professionals who have been discouraged from permitting any emotional or sexual expression on the part of their charges, and have perhaps as it is had too much on their plates looking after their everyday physical needs, are now going to be asked to work out how they stand as far as the sexual lives of their charges is concerned. They are going to have to look more tolerantly and humanely at the fact that the disabled do deserve a measure of emotional and sexual satisfaction, and that to achieve it some of them may behave in a manner contrary to everything the staff have been brought up to accept as right and proper.

It will be difficult, because close contact with other people's emotions probably brings you face to face with considerable personal dilemmas. Staff, for instance, may wonder where it is all going to end. And their problem will be that, if they are going to be expected to encourage deep friendships between residents and help them cope with personal relationships and physical love, the situation may highlight their own emotional problems. If you are a professional working as closely as this with people you are caring for, you may not be able to compartmentalize your own private life, or ignore your own inhibitions, discussing objectively other people's emotional failures and successes. If your husband has gone off you, or your own life is unhappy and lonely, then it is very difficult to advise someone else without a little of your own bitterness and anger rubbing off.

A couple in early middle age, who had been running a hostel for about fifteen years, faced a personal bust-up when the wife gradually went off sex. When one of the residents of the hostel, a man of 42, with a considerable physical handicap, found a girl-friend outside the hostel and went to the warden for contraceptive advice, the warden's own problem came to a head. He felt extremely piqued that, in his own words, 'an unmarried cripple' was getting something he couldn't have. And the strains in his marriage began to affect the whole staff and the atmosphere of the hostel. The warden went so far as to try and thwart the younger man's affair—without success.

In some ways, people in charge of the disabled in residential care give themselves a protective role, shielding their charges like parents. They feel it is their responsibility to protect them from sex and sexuality, partly because they believe the disabled have enough on their plates coping with a disability and partly because they feel that sex is not for them because they are not capable of handling it responsibly. One researcher described a male member of staff who 'frisks the young men's belongings for contraceptives when he suspects something'. So it will be difficult for some to change their deeply ingrained principles, to accept for instance that the disabled in their care should be able to make some decisions for themselves, such as whether to buy contraceptives, or whether to make a pass at another resident. Staff cannot be swept away by new brooms nor can

64

they be forced to take attitudes or perform tasks with which they feel intrinsically uncomfortable. They are, after all, the foundation on which so many establishments are built. But if they are going to find it completely impossible to put into practice some of the new, more humanitarian approaches, and examine their own motives, then quite legitimately they can be accused of putting their own comfort and security before that of their charges.

Many nursing staff in residential care do cope with considerable dignity and sensitivity with, for instance, the problem of male residents' sexual frustrations, because their training has taught them how. Others, however, would be shocked that a man may have an erection while he is being bathed, and horrified at being asked to bring him to orgasm. Yet it is quite a common incident; and if a staff member is not prepared, or is a little unworldly or young, or is frightened by the sight of an erect penis, such a reaction can be terribly distressing for the man. If the nurse feels she cannot perform the function, then being able to talk to the man about why this is so, rather than being shocked and running from the room, can cool the situation and help them both. So staff training should include some basic aspects of sexuality, like the functioning of the body, a woman's sexual needs, an understanding of perversion and the meaning of masturbation.

Group discussion among staff, with or without residents, and counselling for staff, can go a long way to easing embarrassments such as I have illustrated, and help them understand the nature of man's sexuality in a positive rather than a destructive way.

One of the areas that most urgently needs a radical rethink is the belief that the disabled in care should always be bright and cheerful and not cause any trouble. This is despite the fact that many of them are denied that part of their lives that brings many of us great happiness—sex and a deep, lasting relationship with someone of the opposite sex. They are supposed to wear the crown of thorns for society and bear their handicap gladly. But many do not. They hate it. They become frustrated, not only because they are not able to do what everyone else takes for granted, but above all because they do not feel themselves recognized as whole people.

For many members of staff the rewards of their job come

in the form of very loving relationships with the disabled in their care. If the disabled are then encouraged to fall in love, have affairs, with someone else in the home or with an outsider, then staff may feel hurt by this transfer of affection. There is a parallel in the mother/son relationship. When a son grows up he will find a girl to love; and while this love is completely different in kind from the way he feels about his mother, she may bear a grudge, suffer a few pangs of jealousy, because she still has to wash his shirts and mend his socks. In the same way the staff member still has to care for the material needs of the disabled person, even though the latter may have turned to someone else for love; and the helper may feel he is not getting anything in return for his labour. Professionals may have to be helped to grow through this kind of hurt, because it could be difficult to stomach and might be particularly painful when the resident falls out of love and comes running home for comfort and a shoulder to cry on. The staff member can then feel justifiably 'used', if he then has to mop up the tears. The temptation must be to say 'I told you so'; but if the professional can see the situation with tolerance and understanding and accept it as part of life, then both can benefit.

Staff today can no longer have complete control over their residents' lives. Look at the way today's adolescents are challenging the authority of their parents. Out of this is emerging a new sort of relationship, but during the process of change there are catastrophic problems, with talk of the breakdown of law and order and of the structure of the family. The same needs to happen in residential communities. There will be crises of identity, and a shifting in the balance of power; but this is perfectly natural as people adjust themselves to new ideas. It is virtually impossible to bring about change without some upheaval and tears.

Experience has shown, however, that in the residential units where there is a certain level of emotional freedom, where people are encouraged to express themselves sexually, tensions do ease, and arguments, frustrations and temper tantrums do fall off dramatically. This is not to say that life is then a bed of roses, one long sexual Valhalla. New problems do arise. There is always a minority who will abuse freedom, and unwanted pregnancies may have to be dealt with. But experts and social workers at the grass roots, with experience of this new-found freedom, are in no doubt that the easing of restrictive practices, a loosening of the Puritan grip where it is accompanied by open discussion and enlightened staff attitudes, has brought in its wake a happier, more balanced community with residents acting with responsibility and concern for others.

On the whole, the majority of workers involved with the disabled in residential care do accept that the people in their care have got sex problems of one kind or another, just as everyone has sex problems. Some feel it is a Pandora's box they would rather not open. Some are too embarrassed even to look at the situation, and pay only lip-service to a more permissive society. A research worker, after requesting a talk with staff and residents at a home for the physically handicapped, heard a staff member utter this conversation-stopper: 'Now you're all going to talk about you know what, and you're all going to be frank and honest about it.' Such a remark tells you more about the member of staff than about the residents' attitudes to sex, and is not so much a symptom of the insensitivity of the speaker as an attempt on her part to cover up her own shortcomings and fears about sex.

Other professionals deny that sex problems and difficulties with personal relationships exist at all, or are just too busy with all the other problems of running a home like raising funds and finding jobs. Quite recently I approached the warden of a hostel for disabled teenage boys and brought up the subject of their masturbatory and girl-friend problems. He said that the boys were not at all worried about these things. I have rarely met a teenage boy, handicapped or otherwise, who does not have some sort of sexual dilemma. But this warden preferred to ignore this area of his boys' lives. You cannot blame him; he is over-worked, under-staffed and under pressure from outside. But this attitude must surely create extra problems for those in his care.

For the residential home that accepts the need for change, one of the biggest hurdles will be finding the right balance. It is perfectly natural for any community to want to minimize the number of problems it has to tackle day by day, in order to maintain smooth running in the interests of the majority. And a warden would not be human who did not entertain at the back of his mind just the hint of a suspicion that if he lets go the moral reins something might happen that might make it impossible for him to cope without outside help: the nightmarish fantasy of giving an inch and ending up with a brothel on your hands! Again, society's strange attitudes towards sex and disablement would make any warden shiver at the prospect of a public scandal, however exaggerated and unjustified, because he knows how much the situation would be exploited by the media, how much the residents would suffer and staff morale be undermined.

There are, of course, also countless practical barriers to a greater freedom of expression, an enrichment of life, in a residential home. Like money! If we talk about the handicapped having the freedom to express themselves emotionally, they must have the privacy to do it in. And privacy means space and extra facilities. To expect a unit to find the money to spend on expanding facilities, so that each resident can have a room of his own when there are more pressing needs, is laughable in its impracticality. At present single rooms are very single. Dormitories are public places. In sitting rooms and television lounges and recreation rooms you have about as much privacy as in the central concourse at Euston Station. So the shortage of funds and the limitations of existing buildings make it virtually impossible for the most enlightened institutions to provide in practice what they know the disabled need, such as more mixed facilities, less segregation and the privacy that any two people need to get to know each other. In some units sexes are separated even in the workshops. But efforts have got to be made to give residents more privacy to meet and talk intimately, explore mutual feelings and benefit from the refreshment that sexual experience brings, beyond what is possible in communal rooms.

There is, too, the problem of staff interference, which some would call protection, but others might go so far as to describe as nosiness. Some residents in care have complained to me that, even when they can find a bit of privacy and quiet, staff are rarely far away. And they rarely knock on a door before entering. This situation is changing. But how much this is out of deference to our permissive times rather than from a genuine desire to make life happier for the handicapped is debatable.

7

Residential care - residents' problems

No one would deny that every human being has a right to love and be loved, the vulnerable child no less than the hard-headed tycoon, the woman in a wheelchair no less than the Olympic athlete. This is an unassailable fact and really has nothing to do with sex, nothing to do with human weakness. We just need, all of us, to feel wanted and loved for ourselves.

However, for too long it has been assumed that crippled limbs, or lack of sight, or confinement to crutches have been enough to abolish these emotional needs and the desire to love and be loved—particularly if your confinement is in a residential home surrounded by the loving care of professional staff. Yet the handicapped person whose life is spent in residential care has as great a need as anyone, if not a greater need, because he cannot draw his self-respect and self-esteem from a job of work, or a home of his own, or a beautiful garden. And given the opportunity he has the same capacity for adult love as the next man.

But do not let us kid ourselves that we just have to change the attitudes of the staff of residential units and the way will be clear for the disabled to lead a fuller, happier, life with sex as part of it. The moral standards of the residents themselves are likely to be as varied as in any section of the community, running the full gamut from Victorian repressiveness to total anarchy. Attitudes have changed considerably for all of us over the last fifteen years or so, and many people today find themselves accepting views they could not or would not have considered a decade ago. But there is a whole huge grey area, sometimes referred to as the ubiquitous silent majority who, on these topics, are not sure what they think.

This is not fence-sitting through ignorance. It does not necessarily mean they have not thought about it. They say that they are just confused by the rapidity of change today. Many of us are. And in residential homes this silent majority may go no further in expressing their fears than to prefer not to be dragged into situations they either have chosen to ignore or did not know existed in the first place, such as a homosexual affair or adult masturbation.

Clearly this applies to the older generation particularly, but it does seem that the disabled, because of their generally sheltered environment and narrow educational and social experience, tend to lag behind their contemporaries in accepting new ideas and points of view. How much this view of life is reinforced by lack of exposure to current trends, and how much it is just a defence mechanism is discussed in an earlier chapter. But whatever the reason it does follow that they might find it difficult initially to take a balanced view of new approaches to their sexuality as a group, and might, in fact, be shocked by a permissive policy at the top of an organization, especially where new blood, highly trained and progressive, has been brought in to drag that organization into the last quarter of the twentieth century.

So how change is brought about, and at what pace, must depend not just on the people at the top, but on the disabled themselves, if the aim is to help them to be more self-determining. Obviously this pace must depend also on the potential level of maturity of the disabled, their ability to understand, and on the extent to which they have already been deprived of any powers of decision making. You cannot suddenly wake up one morning and tell someone who has always been dressed and bathed to get on with it himself, just as you cannot force someone overnight to start talking about masturbation. It is a process that will take deep understanding, careful counselling and wide open discussion between parents, staff, management committees and the residents.

Parents, of all people, are probably the least eager for change where it concerns their offspring. Many parents find it difficult enough to accept and acknowledge their children's sexuality. Once they do this, they have to accept that their children are becoming adults; and this is difficult. If anything goes wrong within a residential unit, parents are likely to come down like a ton of bricks on the institution to which they have entrusted the welfare of their child, because they expect standards far higher than even they would be able to achieve under their own roofs.

In the search for solutions let us look first at why people go into residential care.

There are those who are so severely handicapped that they cannot be looked after at home. Others may have parents who are reaching an age when they feel they can no longer give their children the care they would want. As we have mentioned in an earlier chapter, women who give birth late in life have a higher risk of producing a handicapped child, so there will be people who have to move into residential care quite early. And there is a third group who will be better looked after in a residential unit than at home where, for financial reasons, or because of the personality of the parents or the demands of the other children in the family, there would be fewer opportunities for training and socializing.

Whatever brings about the separation, it can be traumatic for both sides. Parents may feel a sense of failure, children (of whatever age) may fear they have been rejected. Both emotions are strong, even when it is clear to everyone that a move to residential care is going to improve the quality of life for everyone.

Happily, changing attitudes within residential care are beginning to offer to the handicapped a measure of independence within a framework of caring that many of them would never be able to achieve at home. They have the chance to stand on their own two feet, often for the first time. One girl I know went into a residential hostel after a social worker told her mother she was not giving her daughter enough chance to do things for herself and lead her own life. At least the quality of life in residential homes and hostels no longer heralds the beginning of the end for those who enter.

While there is going to be a wide range of ages among the disabled entering care, the handicaps themselves will vary considerably in their severity. This may make life more complicated for those attempting to encourage self-determination and maturity, for the disabled can be extremely vulnerable if they have experienced rejection and psychological neglect.

So I am not saying to residential homes, that everyone

71

should be given the freedom to hop in and out of bed with whomever they please, because this will obviously not be appropriate for the majority. In a residential home, especially for the severely handicapped and the old, holding hands will probably be as much as they need or want in their friendships. Anything more would be against their nature and inclination. But if they have the need for sexual expression, then they should be able to carry on and count on the help of staff; otherwise the frustrations could be very fragmenting for the community as a whole. What we want to try and avoid is the kind of unhappiness brought about by situations such as have been described to me by staff and social workers: stories of couples courting in out-houses and laundry rooms, of liaisons that had gone on for years in secret, and the lengths to which some couples went to conceal their hand-holding and other intimate contact for fear of official castigation.

A medical superintendent in charge of a large institution tells of a woman who came to him distraught. She had been in the home for thirty years and had a steady relationship with a male resident. For most of the time they had slept together in a disused boiler room. Now the man had died. Staff had known the couple were good friends but none would admit to knowing they were intimate. Another couple, one of whom was in a wheelchair, arranged their rendezvous in a bathroom because only there was there room for the vehicle. Their intimacies were limited to mutual mastur-bation, one of them using a toe because hands could not cope; but they achieved a level of understanding and satisfaction which made life worth living for them. Before that, they had only experienced love from people who had to care for them. But had they been able to express this other love overtly too, how much richer their lives would have been. Each one of these situations is a little human tragedy which could have been avoided had the atmosphere been right for the open expression of love and caring.

Obviously an endless corridor of private suites marked 'for lovers only' is not going to solve any of these personal dilemmas. Although such a suggestion is overstating the case, anything of that nature which puts the disabled on display would probably be so intimidating that it would put anyone off sex for ever, and do more harm than good. It would give

72

sex and sexuality an inflated importance, and take them out of the context of everyday living, which is surely where we want to keep them if we are to achieve the all-important balance we have been talking about. Above all, the handicapped in the more enlightened residential homes will not want to be the guinea pigs of the new permissiveness, forced to accept sexual *mores* they feel uncomfortable with, or trapped into attempting to achieve a degree of sexual satisfaction well beyond their capabilities or desires.

Nevertheless privacy, so much taken for granted by the able-bodied as an integral part of the development of a loving relationship, is vital if people in homes and hostels are to be able to get more out of life. When a resident begins to court, or falls in love, or simply makes friends with someone of the opposite sex, everybody knows about it. This happens in all walks of life. But for the non-handicapped there is escape to the back row of the cinema, to a park bench or restaurant. For the handicapped, especially those in care, these bolt holes are not available. Every new liaison, every exploratory glance and touch comes under the microscope. It is natural curiosity. Some onlookers will be happy about it, others may be jealous or interfering; but by and large they will take more interest in the lovers' progress than would the friends and associates of a couple in the outside world, because it is of more significance to them. Worse still, should the friendship come to an end, there will be whispered inquests, and the couple will have still to live in the same close proximity under the enquiring gaze of everyone else. You would have to be very thick-skinned or very much in love to endure that amount of curiosity, however well-meaning—unless you happened to be like the couple a social worker described to me who never stopped talking about their sexual exploits, and even invited other residents into their room to watch them having intercourse!

To avoid these extremes of behaviour—from secrecy to exhibitionism—staff and residents will have to have the opportunity to express any concern they may feel, voice their own inhibitions and fears, and express any feelings of disgust or revulsion at their fellow residents' behaviour. This sort of discussion may ease the enormous build-up of tensions that can happen in a closed community. Anyone lucky enough to have lived a relatively stable family life

73

knows the kind of knife-edge atmosphere one small altercation can cause between the average family. In a larger community of, say, fifty people it is potentially explosive and not so easy to defuse.

As we start to examine solutions, communication between staff and residents must come top of the list in breaking down barriers of reticence, and introducing new ideas and techniques. This can only be done by putting as much emphasis on the social work understanding of staff as on their nursing ability. Care means not just an endless supply of fresh sheets and the right pills at the right time, but a ready ear and a sympathetic shoulder.

In defining a middle course between permissiveness and restraint, there are going to be innumerable side tracks. After all everyone has his own ideas about what is permissive and what is not. But most would agree that the fear of exploitation of the disabled, vulnerable as they often are, must be a prime concern, especially in residential homes which already have a reputation for open mindedness on the question of residents' friendships. Casual visitors who provide outside services may at some time be tempted to take advantage of a situation, and hurt a young resident. At the same time, though, any 16- or 18-year-old girl can fall prey to the overtures of a married man. She does not have to be handicapped to get trapped, and hurt.

The question that must be asked, with a bearing on the age of consent and the age of majority, is to what extent a staff member, matron or warden, should interfere and advise as well as control. Does the fact that a girl is physically handicapped mean that her status as a decision-making adult is lessened in the eyes of the law? It is a difficult problem. Nevertheless disabled people need to be allowed to make judgments for themselves, where their own personal friendships and relations are concerned.

Some authorities are worried about relationships developing between staff and residents. Some homes lay down rules that this must never happen. In some instances staff have been sacked and residents transferred because of the allegedly disruptive nature of such a friendship. But this is a sweeping judgment. You surely cannot say with any finality that a relationship between two people will always be contrary to the interests of the rest of the community. Each case must be judged individually. There will obviously be instances where a partnership is doomed; but, just as in the outside world, can you encourage a couple to accept this judgment before they have put it to the test? A warden did describe to me the case of a physically handicapped girl with a high I.Q. who married a volunteer in the unit. They went to live a new life outside; but eventually the girl returned to the institution because she found her husband to be a lot less intelligent than she was herself, and the whole relationship unsatisfactory. Maybe staff could have told her this beforehand. But it could well be that the girl was willing to take her chances, as we all do when we marry, and when it failed, emerged the better for the experience, and would not have missed it for worlds. Easier divorce, and at least a freer attitude towards relationships without the marriage contract, can help prevent some of this unhappiness and strife.

However, the possibility of staff falling in love, or having affairs, with residents is a particular boundary that it may not be appropriate for most to cross. The mere fact that one person is in the position of caring for the other may make it very easy indeed for both of them to imagine they are in love, without realizing that this caring and being cared for is a different sort of love—not necessarily the basis for marriage or a lasting relationship. To allow total freedom may possibly be damaging to the majority in a community. For instance if a helper falls in love with one resident and then a second, other residents will be very dubious about how they treat the helper, fearful of trusting their bodily needs to him or her. So this could prejudice someone's chances of being an adequate carer in the future. It is confusing for everyone because the boundaries are being blurred.

Two disabled people married and living independently in the outside world may have enormous problems. For two people married but still living in care, there are other difficulties to be coped with. At present there are few facilities for married couples to make the best of their time together and to live as a twosome. This is one of the reasons staff give for discouraging a relationship from going that far. A few couples have been lucky enough to move into self-contained accommodation, but this is exceptional. One couple I met in a home had been married for three months but had not been able to sleep together, because there was no double bed available, and nowhere one could be put. They were obviously too disabled to lie side by side in a single bed, never mind make love there. Their time together was spent in one or other of their single rooms.

Some experts consider it wise for couples who have met and matched in one home or hostel to transfer to another when they marry, to give them the chance to start a new life. This may have benefits for the young, but would be a little cruel for an older couple, who may have made many friends over the years in their home.

Many people in residential care, especially those who are young, have told me quite categorically that they do not want a boy- or girl-friend in their unit. They want a friendship like everyone else, in which you see each other perhaps two or three times a week. Otherwise with a friend inside the unit, they say, there is no sense of occasion, when you spend an evening together and everyone else can watch the progress of the friendship. For this reason I believe a lot of people in care put a shell around themselves, remaining cool and aloof to protect themselves from intrusion into their emotions; and this is understandable. Such barriers should not be broken down too forcibly, because there are good reasons for them. But unless such a resident has opportunities for outside contact, the mobility to take a walk in the streets or to get a job away from the home, he or she may be very lonely.

Encouraging the participation of the outside world in the life of a home or hostel sounds like a possible solution, but it is easier suggested than done. A hostel in the Midlands which wanted to go further than inviting the public to bring-and-buy sales, opened its dances to the young of the neighbourhood. But it had very little response—probably, the warden suggested, because people are still frightened by disablement and frightened of being patronizing, while the disabled themselves were a little edgy. The warden said he was going to persevere, because he believed the community had a lot to gain from contact with weaker individuals than themselves, and vice versa.

Pre-marital counselling is accepted as invaluable for most engaged couples these days. It may be especially useful for the disabled where a couple appears to be so handicapped that normal marital relations seem impossible. But counsellors and staff have to tread very carefully. One warden tells of the first couple in her unit to marry, who were extremely offended when asked how they were going to manage. They might have been quite justified in taking this frosty attitude. On the other hand it is not unheard-of for couples with a disability to marry and yet not consummate the marriage because they needed help and yet dared not ask for it.

Perhaps in many of these cases more emphasis should be put on the development of worthwhile relationships, and less on marriage itself as the socially acceptable culmination of such an arrangement. In some residential units couples are recognized as 'married' although nothing has been put in writing, and whether they have regular sex or not is left to them. The couples are allowed freely to move around hand-in-hand, to all intents and purposes paired, without censure or comment.

When it comes to the delicate question of whether physical help should be offered by a third party to the handicapped, so that they can achieve sexual satisfaction, there is a great deal of heated debate. There are obviously few who would want this, and fewer professionals willing to give it. But it might be the solution for a tiny minority in care. For instance, a couple may have difficulty getting into a position where they can begin to caress, and may need to be lifted to lie side by side. Couples may even need help to achieve penetration or withdrawal. If such help is given, there is of course the danger that they may come to rely too heavily for help on one individual, who might not always be—or want to be—available.

This problem, and the problem of how far one person can or should help another to masturbate, makes it necessary to ask ourselves very personal and sometimes embarrassing questions; for it must raise the issue of how far it is possible for one individual to take part in another's sexual activity without actually becoming involved himself. If we are totally honest with ourselves, we shall probably admit that the feedback or job satisfaction in many work situations is an important element in helping us carry out sometimes unpleasant tasks. Most of us in the caring professions do our work not only because people need us, but also because we have a deep need of our own to care for and nurture others.

But the professional ethic enables us to keep this in perspective, so that at any time the needs of the patient or client remain paramount. We ought to be able to maintain this perspective when it comes to the question of meeting the sexual needs of the disabled; but social and legal taboos unfortunately intervene, making the whole situation both extremely complicated and somewhat dangerous.

Most women find it fairly easy to give themselves sexual pleasure and relief from tension if necessary without involving anyone else. Many disabled men, however, may find that they cannot do this without help; and if they happen to be under 21, and if the help is given by a man, there may be unpleasant legal consequences. A social worker has been gaoled for masturbating a boy resident in a hostel. Clearly, in this case, the judgment was made on the assumption of deliberate exploitation, when in fact the professional may well have been offering a humane service. In another case, one resident took cigarettes from his fellow, as payment for masturbating him, and half way through would stop and demand more cigarettes before continuing to a climax. Many men climax while being washed or bathed; this is usually considered to be entirely normal, but it may be a frightening experience for a helper or nurse who is totally unprepared.

So that helpers can get their own feelings into perspective, there should be adequate opportunity in every residential home for staff discussion. Problems can then be looked at and examined, and anxieties understood. It is particularly necessary that there should be some degree of corporate responsibility taken for any action that might be considered at all unusual, so that no individual can ever be arraigned without support.

Increasing consultation between staff and residents has, in many homes, gone a long way towards easing some of the unnecessary tensions and creating a more egalitarian society; and it has helped those on both sides to appreciate some of each other's problems.

Some homes and hostels have also made arrangements for groups of residents to meet a counsellor, and this has provided an extra opportunity to explore feelings and discuss fears and frustrations. Staff may be afraid that tales are being told behind their backs, without their having any chance to defend themselves; and they may also feel usurped, particularly if they think that residents are opening their hearts and minds to someone with whom they have only a nodding acquaintance. But this is the very basis of the success of services like the Marriage Guidance Council, where people can take their problems, if they want to, to someone who isn't in any way connected with them. Of course it must be clear in everyone's mind that the counsellor is there to supplement the staff, and not to take over their problem-solving role.

Counsellors act as a sounding-board; and they can help people see a situation more clearly precisely because they are not involved emotionally, are not there to pass judgment, and have no axes to grind. Many wardens have found that residents are remarkably willing to talk freely about themselves and their personal problems to staff or counsellors, without any compulsion. The most important thing about outside counselling is simply that it should be available for those who want it. For instance, a counsellor may be able to help a couple by making arrangements for them with the warden for the provision of proper sleeping accommodation, where they might have been nervous of asking a staff member themselves; he may also help by arranging for them to be given adequate contraceptive advice. One counsellor spent several sessions with a middle-aged spastic woman who had been deeply upset by the marriage of her closest friend. Another counsellor worked for months with a disabled couple who wished to marry and leave the hostel, helping them to understand the nature of their commitment to each other.

Sex education itself may be part of the counselling process, especially among the young in care. It has a chapter to itself in this book, so suffice it to say here that, even if it appears that sex education is not absolutely necessary for, say, the severely handicapped, this does not mean that it should be ignored.

An adjunct to this is the question of contraception and contraceptive education. Many disabled women look to pregnancy as a demonstration of their femininity, which they might find difficult to express in other ways; and they may deliberately go out of their way to conceive for this reason and no other. Married couples might see children as a proof to the world of their consummated partnership. These motives can be harmful, and often it is only by open discussion that it is possible for them to begin to understand how mistaken are these ideas.

So contraceptive education and the availability of contraceptives to the unmarried, as well as the married, in care is just as essential as it is for the community in general. It does not, as scaremongers love to try and point out, necessarily increase promiscuity or disrupt family life. On the contrary it can release couples from needless fear and worry. Contraceptives are freely available now, so there is no reason why the handicapped should be denied them. And this means free availability where the handicapped can reach them: not just in inaccessible barbers' shops, not at F.P.A. clinics a bus-ride away, but in the homes themselves through doctors and counsellors, from staff and even from slot-machines.

Homosexual relationships are usually viewed very tolerantly in single sex homes; and this is as it should be, because for some couples such a friendship may be all that is available to them, and may provide comfort and consolation in an otherwise lonely world. Naturally, the feelings of other residents have to be taken into consideration; but, again, counselling can help to ease disgust or embarrassment. It is likely that residents tend to be less heterosexual than people outside, because of their limitations of choice; but, whichever way they turn, they must surely be allowed the same freedoms under the law as the rest of society.

Finally let us examine another adjunct to sex education and the atmosphere in which it is explored—that of pornography and the availability of books and magazines, maybe even films, which not only explore sex and sexuality, but go one step further into the area of deviation. This may be totally unacceptable to some. Nevertheless, just as pornography is available to people in the street, so it should be left to the free choice of the individual in care whether he or she acquires it. There is evidence that many men get considerable satisfaction from reading this literature, when little else in the way of sexual expression is available to them, just as women may get satisfaction from romantic novels and magazines.

In this chapter there may well be a great deal that will offend and disgust those who have worked for decades with the

80

handicapped. They may feel themselves qualified to dismiss as trivial or dangerous some or all of the suggestions and observations. But equally, staff and other professionals who have experienced an easing of those strict moral standpoints, know that in its wake emerges a happier community with fewer tensions and fewer frustrations. The important thing is to raise the level of awareness and understanding of these problems, and so to help the disabled to make decisions for themselves, and give residents and staff alike a little more insight into each other's lives.

8

Sex education for the handicapped

Sex education for what? This is the question parents wrestle with when they reach that awkward juncture in their handicapped child's life when the facts of life have to be told.

The amount of sex education the average British schoolchild receives is derisory. Parents leave it to the teachers and teachers assume that parents will provide it. In the end many children finish up with their heads filled with a mixture of pure biology and birds-and-bees mythology. Nothing has been mentioned of sexuality, personal identity or human relationships.

For the handicapped child in a special school or in residential care the subject is even more neglected. But at least in this case the neglect is understandable. Parents and teachers often feel that if a child's chances of a normal married life with a family are slender then there is no point in whetting the appetite by giving him a sex education he is not going to be able to put to proper use; better to withhold the information and ignore the subject in the hope that it will go away, and content the child with the facts of the reproductive system of the common frog.

Apart from being unrealistic, this attitude reinforces once more the theory that the handicapped are not quite human, and presupposes that they, unlike the rest of society, can do without sex as long as it is denied them. This is cruel and contemptuous and can cause a great deal of personal suffering for the handicapped child and adolescent in particular.

The disabled child is exposed daily to sexual propaganda in films, television, books and magazines and from poster hoardings, and he or she is also aware of the sometimes quite disturbing changes taking place in his or her body, with the onset of wet dreams and menstruation. Their natural curiosity is no different from that of able-bodied children, so they will want to know why these things are happening and what they mean.

To discourage emerging sexual feelings with disapproval or a blind eye, to cover them up as unimportant subjects nice people do not talk about, is quite likely not only to make the child more curious and determined to find the answers somehow, but also to fill him with feelings of guilt. After all there must be some reason why those around him are trying to hide the facts. On the one hand he is bursting to know what it is all about, and on the other he has a sneaking feeling he should not be thinking these thoughts at all anyway. The contradiction is enough to confuse anyone. But if the able-bodied child finds himself thwarted in this way he can always seek the information elsewhere. He has the mobility which enables him to go to other sources, such as libraries, cinemas and, above all, friends, to compare notes and to observe others' behaviour. The disabled child has to look to his immediate surroundings which are usually hemmed in by adult figures.

Yet if these sexual manifestations can be discussed as normal functions of the human body, in the context of growing up and becoming adult, at least the disabled child will be able to identify with his able-bodied peers and share an area of his life which actually *is* functioning normally and is no different from what is happening to all other children.

One of the major problems—and one which troubles many teachers—is who provides the sex education? Most teachers would agree that it is too important a subject to risk leaving to parents. In an ideal world they would be the best people to impart the facts of life, as part of family life; but many of them feel that they are hopelessly inadequate, and therefore are often reluctant to raise the subject with their own children. They can manage the biology bits, but when it comes to sexual intercourse, and how babies are born, and their own role as mothers and fathers, their own emotional hang-ups and inhibitions (the result perhaps of their own patchy acquaintance with the facts of life as children) intervene. Their child's emotional dependence on them causes embarrassment, and their unwillingness to accept that their child is capable of sexual feelings may make the whole subject fraught.

Many handicapped children are not too keen on hearing it from their parents anyway! Questioned about who they thought most suitable to impart the facts, many expressly plumped for outsiders with whom they have no ordinary day-to-day contact. They said they felt too emotionally involved with teachers and medical helpers who might know them intimately, and who probably handled their bodies in the course of everyday care.

Many professionals caring for the handicapped—social workers, teachers, psychologists, doctors and therapists—have never considered sex education within their scope. They either feel unable to cope or quite justifiably say they have not the time. Yet they above all, observing each child day by day, must realize how vital sex education is.

The skill needed to handle this delicate and difficult job means that there is inevitably a shortage of the right kind of people. But many teachers do have an enormous capacity for adapting themselves to new circumstances. Remember how the old-style maths teachers managed to change to new maths without too much trouble. So the right person can probably be found who will not only be acceptable to the children (most important) but will also give them a sex education that both spans the facts of life and offers an opportunity to understand personal relationships. This could explore, among many other subjects, feelings between parents and children or brothers and sisters, discuss the meaning of jealousy within a family, and give an insight into the significance of their own friendships.

There are problems. A married woman with three healthy children of her own agreed to take a class of handicapped thirteen-year-olds in sex education, and told me how distressing she found the job. 'I found it depressing because their expectations seemed so unreal. Their chances of marriage in my eyes were very small, yet they had high hopes of husbands and wives and children. I thought of my own kids and the opportunities they were going to have, and I felt sad—over-privileged. The tendency in these circumstances is to go along with them, protect them from reality, boost their expectations rather than disillusion them. Yet I realized I wasn't helping them, because between themselves they were going to talk; and if they had any intelligence at all—and they did have—they would know deep down what they could expect and what was fantasy.'

So in a way handicapped children need more sex education than ordinary children, not less; and because there is often less pressure on their curriculum, it should be possible to incorporate it on a long-term basis throughout the school years—from 8 to 15, perhaps, using a variety of classes and presentations from biology and literature to social studies and home economics.

One important aspect of the child's development, from both teachers' and parents' points of view, is how much opportunity can be given for the child to express normal, healthy rebellion against accepted standards and *mores*. Able-bodied children do this easily enough, because they have the freedom to shout and insult and run, offend and take the punishment, be abusive and laugh it off. It is not easy to punish a handicapped child, physically or psychologically, for a misdemeanour, because the person administering the cane or the extra homework or the deprivation, feels he is adding to the pain the child already suffers daily with the disability. Yet rebellion is normal and healthy; and if youngsters do not have the chance to rebel and argue and offend, they may leave it till later, when they have formed a more lasting relationship, and then try to play out their adolescent rebellion with their partner, with destructive results.

Today the greater freedom of discussion offered by the permissive society to explore subjects which were previously taboo can be a positive help to the handicapped, *if* they are allowed and encouraged to use this freedom for their own particular needs. It may be difficult in a church-sponsored home, in a school supported by a charity with older-generation governors, or where parents are looking censoriously over teachers' shoulders, to establish the freedom of speech necessary for the kind of environment where children can have the self-confidence to express their real feelings. The public reputation of the establishment may override the needs of the children, when the question of sex education arises. But children need to be encouraged to talk about their feelings, about their hopes and fears for their future prospects, and to express in words among their peers how they see their handicap and how much difference it makes to them and to their way of life.

They need to explore, with the help and support of a teacher, their relationship with their parents, what they think their parents expect of them, whether they feel smothered by mother-love, how much freedom they think they should have, and whether their parents should allow them to take risks. Do they prefer parents who want them in at 9 o'clock because they are concerned for their safety, or would they rather have parents who do not care what hour they come in? Do they feel a burden to their parents? How long do they envisage living with them? All these things need discussion, in fact everything about the future pattern of their lives, and particularly whether they might lead a fuller life in residential care. In a way it is group therapy, because they will see their friends in similar dilemmas to themselves, with the same worries and hopes. This open discussion can begin to help them achieve a balanced view of their disability, and accept the reality of their own situation. There must, of course, be a suitable person to guide the discussion, who can help to moderate expectations without dimming or censoring them.

The facts of life themselves should be given in the context of human relationships and simple psychology. The children need to see that sex, heterosexual or homosexual, is something to be enjoyed, but also something which involves responsibility and caring. It must be related to their everyday lives, so that they can understand what 'being turned on' means, and the significance of the attraction between themselves and others. Many boarding and day schools for the handicapped discourage pupils from even holding hands, afraid of what might follow. Yet this simple human contact can be very satisfying for the young, and, backed up with discussion and counselling about every individual's responsibility to himself and to others, need hold no particular threat to the community.

The handicapped child needs a tremendous amount of help with the practical problems of his or her emerging sexuality. Handicapped girls for instance, especially those with crippled limbs or confined to wheelchairs, may find great difficulty in coping with menstruation and sanitary protection. The onset of a first period can be a traumatic experience. It is also a very private experience. The girl with a disability needs a great deal of preparatory consultation so that she can begin to cope with the sheer gymnastics of the thing. Boys who are disabled may not have the mobility to mop up after their wet dreams; and if they have not been prepared for it, and reassured that this is normal functioning of the human body, they may imagine they have been wetting the bed, and become guilt ridden and afraid that parents or residential staff will be shocked.

At the same time, children must have the opportunity to talk among themselves, to go through as nearly as possible the same growing-up processes as ordinary children. Experiences in school and street, in secret corners and behind bushes, through the phases of dirty jokes and crushes, of touching and caresssing each other, are the things which tell a child how others respond, and how we each relate to others. The handicapped child given these opportunities will learn far more from his peers than from the adult world.

In this way the handicapped young will begin to understand themselves and their roles as boys or girls. They will learn to relate to the opposite sex in general, realizing that sex and sexuality are not just to do with intercourse, the bedroom and the maternity ward, but with our self image, the way we are able to mix in society and get on with other people, and how others see us.

All this can lead on to discussion about such questions as whether you are still a man if you are not a breadwinner or a property owner (today's manly status symbols), which many handicapped boys may never be, or whether you can be a real woman if you remain childless. Fortunately new attitudes to the roles of men and women (with men helping in the home and women earning high salaries) are helping to free the handicapped from the straightjacket of traditions which previously made them feel under-privileged and second class. Increasingly today they can retain their masculinity and femininity without the traditional sexual symbols.

There is also a whole range of ancillary questions which need to be discussed between children and their mentors, such as sex without marriage (a tricky one for any parent or teacher these days); illegitimacy; society's responsibilities to the unmarried mother; promiscuity; perversion; and whether coitus, the traditional goal of sexual union, should be accepted as such without question of alternative—especially as many handicapped people will never achieve it, and therefore need to know that 'there are more ways than one to skin a cat'!

Handicapped children sometimes appear to be slow to mature in comparison with their non-handicapped contemporaries. Yet in truth their rate of maturation is more likely to depend on those around them than on any other factor. They often have much higher moral standards than their peers; but this is only because they do not receive quite the same exposure to current trends in permissiveness, prevented as they are from mixing with a wide cross-section of their own generation. Additionally they may use a certain puritanism as a protection from having to cope with their sexual feelings, and put on a veneer of moral indignation and prudishness to shield themselves from situations they would like to be involved with, but which frighten them because of their own feelings of inadequacy—but they share this tendency with able-bodied youngsters from restrictive backgrounds.

Society's still quite strongly held view that love means marriage means children, should be put under the microscope to see whether alternatives might provide the same amount of satisfaction and happiness. Many disabled girls do want children desperately because they feel, as people with a degree of helplessness themselves, that they will appear less helpless compared with a baby. Exercising a relative amount of power over the baby makes them seem more adult. They may always have been on the receiving end of care: now they want something to care *for*. The way to help them is not to prevent them having friendships with the opposite sex at all, but to give them the opportunity to examine their motivations and see how difficult it really would be to bring up a child. If they remain childless then the decision will at least have been theirs, and it will have been an adult one.

Fortunately there is less stigma attached to being childless today. Once upon a time it was thought to be anti-social and selfish. Neighbours would scoff at a childless couple. But today, with the world population explosion out of all proportion to world food resources, it is recognized that we do not need everyone to have babies; to be childless from choice actually benefits society. So by choosing not to have children, a disabled woman or couple need no longer feel second class or incomplete. After all, many able-bodied women make the same choice today.

A common dilemma for people caring for handicapped adolescents arises in helping them talk about the sometimes strongly felt desire to marry someone able-bodied: at the back of their minds is the wild hope that one day they will be 'cured', in which case they would not want to be lumbered with a handicapped partner. Others feel that if they marry someone else with a handicap it somehow makes them even more handicapped. But the reality of the situation is that many disabled couples make very happy marriages because of the understanding they have of each other's handicap, and because their relationship is based on communication and not on any element of pity. This is not to say that 'mixed' marriages do not work. But if young people can first work through these feelings of wanting to be made more 'whole' by being married to someone unhandicapped, then they can make the 'right' decision for the 'right' reasons when the time comes. They can examine their motives a little more clearly. Introduced to them in the course of sex education discussion, a disabled couple with or without children could be a marvellous 'visual aid' towards an understanding of what is reality and what is not.

I have been emphatic throughout this book that sex without marriage may be a solution in many cases for the disabled, as it is for the able-bodied. Society is beginning to realize that, although some people are not lucky enough to find the right marriage partner, this does not mean that they have to be condemned to a life of celibacy. So let those who never meet up with Mr or Miss Right still enjoy the pleasures and satisfactions of sex. This applies particularly to the disabled, because there is no point in keeping yourself 'pure' for a marriage partner who may never turn up. But when this subject comes up for discussion among young people in the course of sex education classes, it should never be taken out of the context of caring, even though tokens like wedding bells and gold rings are not going to enter into it. I would go so far as to say that love itself need not be present in such a relationship; but caring should always be there. To have a good sex relationship, there needs to be an element of sharing and knowing you are appreciated for what you are.

When we talk about sex education for the handicapped, we are being totally unrealistic if we confine ourselves to a discussion of marriage, children, non-reproductive sex, loving and caring, because for so many handicapped people none of this will be relevant, perhaps due to severe disability or isolation. This is why sex education for the disabled so often needs to go much further, and scan wider horizons of experience, than for the average child with every chance of marrying happily and having children.

Masturbation is part of growing up for any adolescent girl or boy, handicapped or otherwise. Statistics say that most boys and about a third of girls masturbate in their youth; but whatever the figures, children should grow up understanding that there is nothing dirty about it, that it is simply a part of emerging sexuality, a learning process. The handicapped, however, may find that because of the limitations their handicap imposes, masturbation is the only physical release they will ever have. They need to understand that, if this is the case, there is nothing to worry about, that it does not damage the health or make you go blind. One boy told his teacher that he believed that if you masturbated you couldn't have children. Which in one sense is true, but he did not mean it that way! The handicapped boy or girl needs to see that this private activity is not offensive, and that if it brings satisfaction and relief it is justified and acceptable. At the same time, though, let it be stressed that masturbation must nearly always be second best and should not be substituted on a regular basis where a caring relationship between two people is possible, unless of course mutual masturbation is adopted as a solution for two where intercourse is either difficult or impossible for physical or psychological reasons.

Homosexuality is often a stage in the growing experience of the adolescent; and, since one in twenty of the population is thought to be this way inclined, then it follows that among the handicapped there will be some homosexuals. For some people an understanding of the nature of homosexuality will help towards the solving of problems of loneliness and isolation. It may be rather frightening at first, but explanation of it as in part an extension of crushes and passions may at least release some of the secret guilt which people nurture when they realize they are fond of someone

90

of the same sex. The questions of the rightness or wrongness, the normality or abnormality, of behaviour like homosexuality and masturbation, should again be worked through in the course of discussion so that the handicapped adolescent can see the alternatives open to him and make a decision in the light of the climate of opinion among his peers and mentors.

All this information about sex and sexuality is for nothing if it is not backed up with practical advice about contraception, abortion, and sterilization. But contraception should be discussed in positive not negative terms: it *must* not be another way for the teacher (and, by proxy, society) to say 'you are handicapped, so you must not have children, therefore use contraceptives'. This is hurtful and useless. It should be explained that no couple should have a child unless they have positively decided it is right for them. With contraception almost 100 per cent sure today, everyone has this choice.

What the handicapped need, as well as knowing it exists, is to understand and understand how to use contraception, and to know how much it costs, where it is bought or acquired, and why some methods are better than others. The young handicapped should be treated like the able-bodied in this respect above all. But also they need the confidence to talk about it, so that if the time comes when they decide to sleep with a boy-friend or girl-friend, they are not frightened of asking for help.

The dangers of venereal disease cannot be ignored. It may be that a handicapped boy who does not have a steady girl-friend will go to a prostitute; so he should know the risks involved and the course to follow if he does contract VD. It is no good parents and teachers throwing their hands up in horror at such a warning. It is a possibility, and boys should be fore-armed.

The availability of good explicit books and films, not necessarily aimed at the handicapped, but for general consumption, will back up all these discussions and open other corridors for debate. There are a considerable number of really good films and books available today for the use of teachers and parent groups. Anything that, in the context of loving and caring, shows that deviation and variation is part of everyday life, does some good and can free the handicapped from the conspiracy of silence surrounding sex. Above all they must have the opportunity for individual counselling about their own problems. The value of counselling is being recognized in all fields of social work and it may be particularly helpful for the handicapped child who is too nervous to express himself in class with teachers he knows intimately: he may be willing to open his heart to a caring stranger he can trust, expressing his frustrations and aggressions privately.

This chapter has not discussed specifically the problems of the mentally handicapped as opposed to those with a physical disability, nor has it dealt with the special needs of the deaf and the blind, in learning about sex. What has been said applies to them too. There has been an even stronger argument put forward against sex for the mentally retarded, on the grounds that they are not capable of behaving (handling their sexuality) responsibly. This is a sweeping statement, and could apply as much to the handicapped person's ability to handle the coin of the realm as to his ability to cope with sexual feelings and urges.

The particular problems of the mentally handicapped are discussed in a later chapter. Suffice it to say here that, like the physically disabled, if they are denied information about what is happening in their minds and bodies, and do not have the opportunity to talk about them, society is making the situation of their handicap even worse. I heard of one girl, mentally retarded, who believed that menstruation only happened to her.

Blind children need the extra facility during sex education to learn about the shape and function of the human body. In Sweden they are given the opportunity to touch living naked bodies, both male and female, so that they know something of the anatomy. This sort of enlightened experience would eradicate the situation illustrated by the boy who drew a picture of his mother with her breasts on her back. Plaster models are a reasonable substitute: for instance, a girl who cannot see photographs of an erect penis may avoid a harrowing experience later on if she can feel a model of one.

For deaf children the special need is for plenty of books and films on every aspect of sex because they may not be picking up information by word of mouth from other children.

Amidst all this discussion of the how and the why of sex and sexuality, in school and out, teachers must work closely with parents. Very often parents of handicapped children are already more involved with their children's school than the parents of the able-bodied; but it might help if schools were to set up groups for parents to discuss with teachers and those giving the sex instruction every aspect of their child's sexuality. Parents may need as much help as the children.

The aim of sex education for the handicapped, as for every member of the community, must primarily be to help each individual take responsibility for his own sexual life, and to provide an atmosphere in which the individual can live the kind of sex life he chooses. But because the disabled need acceptance even more than most, and are susceptible to sexual exploitation by those who choose to play on the fact, they need sex education almost as urgently just as a defence. For this reason, and so that the child can get used to it gently, sex education needs to be spread over a number of learning years—and not just suddenly introduced into family conversation or a biology class.

9

Special problems of the mentally handicapped

The last few years have seen an increasing recognition of the mentally handicapped person's ability to live in the community, instead of being locked away out of the sight and out of the mind of society. The mentally retarded are no longer compulsorily hospitalized unless there is strong evidence that they may do themselves damage or that society will be endangered.

This humane understanding of the needs of the mentally handicapped is real progress. However society should not pat itself too warmly on the back, because when we come to discuss sexuality, marriage and child bearing in relation to the mentally handicapped, progress stops. And up goes the cry for compulsory sterilization.

The fearful myth that the mentally sick and subnormal, even more than the physically handicapped, are promiscuous and have voracious sexual appetites which they are incapable of satisfying responsibly or within a socially acceptable pattern of behaviour, is one that still holds water for many; and although statistics keep pouring out to explode the myth, old prejudices and fears die hard. Equally durable is the fallacious belief that mental retardation is hereditary. Both are used as reasons for reproductive limitation.

At one time people spoke about protecting the mentally handicapped 'from the ravages of a cruel and exploitative society'. Concern was mysteriously transferred to the need to protect society from 'the contamination of inferior mental stock and its perpetuation in increasingly large numbers'. Confusing!

So while everything that this book has been saying about the sexual and personal-relationship problems of the handicapped in general applies also to those with a degree of mental retardation, we must accept that there are further difficulties here of some complexity.

First of all, let us examine those myths. A survey of 1,174 mentally handicapped women allowed out of Midlands subnormality hospitals on licence under the old deficiency laws, found that they produced only twenty-five illegitimate children amongst them within twenty years. In the United States, a survey of a large retarded population found an average of slightly more than two children per family, a number slightly less than the national average.

A study in Britain of thirty-six marriages among mentally handicapped people, found that thirty-two couples had remained together for between one and fifteen years, with an average of seven years. Of these thirty-two couples, nineteen were supportive and affectionate, and a further six were moderately happy, although showing some stress. Of the remaining seven couples, there were four in which one member was heavily dependent on the other, and three which were predominantly unhappy. This is a success-rate of twenty-five out of thirty-six, which is very high indeed when measured against marriages in the general population. Fifteen of these thirty-two couples were childless, although within childbearing years; and the remaining seventeen couples had forty children between them. This is an average of 1.5 children, to be compared with the 2.1 expected among normal couples of similar age.

Research has also shown that the severely handicapped have a lower fertility potential, and this is mainly because sexual activity for the human being, unlike animals whose sexual desires are instinctive, requires an element of skill.

In a study published in Britain in 1963, only four of a sample of 1,280 mentally handicapped people were found to have severely handicapped parents. Another estimate of the proportion of handicapped children born to handicapped parents concludes that something like 30 per cent of them will be either severely or mildly handicapped.

In another study published in 1965, it was found that 91 per cent of the children born to mothers certified as mentally deficient under the old acts had normal intelligence. The mother with the lowest I.Q. had the child with the highest I.Q., and, yes, you've guessed, the mother with the highest

I.Q. had the child with the lowest I.Q. But the mothers themselves were well within the range of lower normal intelligence, and for fourty-four of them it was their pregnancy that led to their being certified.

These opinions and statistics have of course to be balanced against what society means by mental handicap at any particular time. Nevertheless studies do seem to prove that the offspring of the mentally retarded need not be intellectually inferior, if appropriate guidance and educational assistance is given. Obviously, these children will be intellectually and socially deprived if they are also deprived of support from outside their family environment. At the same time we cannot overlook the fact that intellectual inadequacy does not always entail social irresponsibility; there are, after all, many people walking the streets who would be classed as highly intellectual, but who are nevertheless quite capable of irrational behaviour.

We can keep repeating these facts and figures, yet some will still find reasons why the mentally handicapped should be denied the same sexual rights as normal people.

In the past, segregation from society was the weapon used to protect the outside world from the sexuality, and thus the reproductive potential, of the mentally subnormal. Women were locked away during their child-bearing years, and then released back into the community when their reproductive years were over. Today this solution is no longer legally possible, although residential homes, hostels and hospitals sometimes maintain a policy of segregation of the sexes for these very same reasons.

A recent survey in Britain found that less than a quarter of the occupational therapy departments in subnormality hospitals in a sample of 300 catered for both sexes. In one hospital, a newly-built occupational therapy department had two separate entrances for men and women, with no connection between the two. In the same hospital, female nurses were not allowed to visit the male workshops without the permission of the matron.

Slowly we are coming to realize that this is a cruel and impractical solution. Research is beginning to show that segregation is counter-productive to any attempt to help the mentally retarded develop adult behaviour. As well as denying them the pleasures and rewards of sex, it often prevents them from taking any active part in the life of the community.

In Sweden tremendous efforts have been made to provide mixed accommodation for the mentally handicapped in residential care. The Swedes involved in these experiments say that adults living in single-sex institutions become childish, egocentric and aggressive, and that there is a great deal of open masturbation. In mixed accommodation, however, where residents can have not only their own rooms but also their own washing facilities and toilets, or at most share with one or two others, behaviour is improved, residents have more consideration for each other, and they are eager to mix with groups beyond their own small world. Adults are allowed to live together, with the women on the contraceptive pill; and homosexual friendships are not frowned upon. One of the net results is a calmer society all round.

Reports from Sweden also say that, where mentally handicapped couples are allowed to live together in institutions, it has become clear that their needs are not so much for full sexual expression as for more gentle contact like kissing, cuddling and sleeping together side by side for warmth and comfort.

This is all a far cry from the myth of uncontrolled and perverted sexual desire. Admittedly the mentally retarded in institutions are convicted from time to time of gross indency, of indecent exposure and of sexual assault. And the news media make the most of it as though there was a plague upon the land. But social workers are sure that this kind of behaviour is the result of an inability to make normal approaches to the opposite sex, which may be due to a combination of long-term segregation, lack of sex education and emotional experience, and deprivation of affection and love in early years. And don't let us forget that there are plenty of so-called normal people who behave like this under stress, just as there are thousands of subnormals whose behaviour never leads to complaint.

It would be wrong to dismiss as anachronistic and inhumane all that has been done for the mentally handicapped to date, without examining closely the very real problems still facing those aiming at greater self determination for the mentally subnormal.

Most workers agree that a large proportion of the mentally handicapped are educable and can be trained. This has already been proved in extensive occupational training schemes, where the handicapped are given the chance to do useful, if humble, tasks in supervised workshops. However, the very dullness of their working routine makes it even more important that their training should not stop at threading beads or packing needles. To know that, after a boring day at a workshop bench, it will be possible to go 'home' to someone who cares, can brighten life beyond measure.

To deny the mentally handicapped these simple human desires and sexual feelings is to place a burden on them too great to cope with, especially if they are exposed to the emancipated, sex-oriented outside world. So whereas it was possible previously to keep them away from sexuality, today it is not only impossible but also positively cruel and unfair. We have to allow them to enjoy sex, because society has changed and because of their own greater freedom. But we have also to give them the tools and the guidelines to cope with the situation, and protection so that they do not get hurt any more than is necessary in the course of normal human contact. A major problem is that they do not always realize the consequences of their actions. They tend to live very much in the present, and sometimes find it difficult to comprehend that A (intercourse) may lead to B (pregnancy) may lead to C (a child).

The tools we need to give them, then, are the understanding of birth control, and the skill to make use of today's foolproof techniques. And this does not mean all-round sterilization. It is too facile an answer, and I would hesitate to make the judgment, or give anyone the power to decide, that certain people are unsuitable for breeding and parenthood and should therefore be sterilized. It is patently obvious that parenthood would be disastrous for certain mentally handicapped people; but it is a dangerous and insidious policy to talk about compulsory sterilization for any whole group.

Reproduction is a basic human right, just as the right to love and be loved is an intrinsic part of the human condition. There are cogent reasons why some people should be sterilized. But the question is who decides who should be and

98

who not? Do you draw the line at a certain I.Q. level? Can society allow such a sweeping infringement of human rights?

It is a sensitive subject, and my own feeling is that it depends on the nature of the handicap, and the circumstances of the individual. For some severely handicapped people it will not apply, because they will not be capable of intercourse: for instance, the warden of one hostel told me of a girl who had insisted on taking the Pill for years, although she and her boyfriend had never managed intercourse because they were never ready at the same time. Others, unable to understand that sex means meeting someone else's needs too, may be capable of intercourse but to gratify only themselves: I know of a girl who has become pregnant twice without really realizing what was happening. Such people can, with help, learn to act in a way that is compatible with living within a community—and this may be quite different from what they would do if left alone.

For the majority of the mentally handicapped, then, the pleasure of sex is their incontestable right; and it is our job, as professionals, to try to help them enjoy sex with responsibility, and to explain the sad consequences of bringing unwanted babies into the world. This may be a difficult task. What do I do when a backward girl comes to me and says she desperately wants a child? Have I the right, after all, to say that she shouldn't? The predicament for society today is that we are more aware of people's rights than we have ever been before; and we have become more conscious than ever before of the ways in which these rights, if left unguarded, can be intruded upon and eroded. Certain intrusions are unacceptable now, because we know and understand more about the feelings and needs of the individual. But if we protect the rights of the individual, then we must protect the rights of these people we call mentally subnormal. Whatever potential they have in life, we are limiting it when we pass judgment and say no sex, no marriage and no child-bearing.

Education and training must be accompanied by contraceptive counselling. There are several reasons why certain methods of contraception are unsuitable for the mentally retarded; but it has been recognized that if a doctor or counsellor establishes a good relationship with an individual woman or a couple they will accept the contraceptive advice, and usually cope quite well with whatever method they select together.

An American survey in 1970, on the supply to the mentally handicapped of the major forms of contraception, suggested that the I.U.D. (despite a higher expulsion rate noticed among the retarded) and the Pill were probably the best choices in the circumstances. The Pill got top billing because it entailed a minimum invasion of privacy, although some people have expressed doubt whether the retarded can be relied upon to take the tablet daily. However, as many mentally subnormal people are quite capable of managing their bodily needs day by day, like dressing and washing, there is no reason to believe that the taking of the Pill could not be part of that routine.

Marriage is certainly a more demanding undertaking than the use of contraception, and although hopefully the two go together they have to be discussed quite separately. Marriage can be particularly rewarding and beneficial to the mentally handicapped: the desire and ability to help someone else, the fact that someone is depending on you, builds self-respect considerably. It has also been found that the skills of two handicapped people together are greater than the sum of their individual skills. They often bring out the best in each other, and they sometimes do much better than expected. This may quite possibly be due to their separation from those on whom they were previously dependent, close families, say, with supporting brothers and sisters; away from them, they do seem to manage to put more into a marriage. It appears that, in these marriages, sex is not always terribly important, because a great deal of energy and effort is used up simply in living together, coping with everyday crises and being considerate and caring. But the success of such a marriage is based on exactly the same principle as that of any other marriage—the *desire* to succeed. The mentally handicapped may do better when they marry over the age of 25—but the same applies to the general marriage situation in England and Wales.

Any professional today advising a married couple with one or both partners subnormal against child-bearing, would probably be objecting not on the grounds of eugenics, but rather because of the difficulties the child would face growing up in such an environment. These difficulties may be

100

economic as well as cultural, particularly if the parents have a small earning capacity. But, whatever the situation, the couple should not be denied the opportunity to talk about their feelings about children, so that any decision they make seems their own, and rational and fair.

There is evidence that mentally handicapped parents do not necessarily face insurmountable problems when they bring up a family. In a recent study, the children of school age from seventeen such families were mostly below average intelligence, and about half according to their teachers showed 'abnormal adjustment'; but none of them made a habit of being away from school to look after younger children or play truant. The pre-school age children in the survey were all well nourished, fairly treated and clean. Six children from three families were in care; eight of the families had had intensive social work help at least over one year. One of the social workers was in no doubt that the time he had spent with his particular family had helped them to grow; and he agreed that it was their right to live in a normal community and draw on the social support available.

A study of parents in the United States found that problems for the mentally handicapped couple were the result more often of poverty than of their handicap. It showed that while 42 per cent of parents were giving 'satisfactory' care to their children, 32 per cent gave 'questionable' care and 26 per cent 'unsatisfactory' care. There seemed to be no significant relationship between the mother's intelligence and the quality of care the children received; but it did seem that over a third of the parents giving 'satisfactory' care had an adequate income, and only 8 per cent 'inadequate'. In the groups giving 'questionable' and 'unsatisfactory' care, none had an adequate income.

I have already discussed in the foregoing chapters the fear of exploitation that bothers many people involved with the handicapped. It is a real problem, even though there is legislation aimed at protecting the mentally retarded. Under the 1956 Sexual Offences Act (Section 7), it is an offence for a man to have intercourse with a woman he knows to be or suspects of being severely subnormal. Under Section 128 of the 1959 Mental Health Act, it is an offence for a member of staff of a hospital or home to have intercourse with a patient. There is no doubt that there are people capable of taking advantage of the feeble-mindedness of others. Yet some of the blame for these incidents must fall on the shocking lack of sex education and general emotional support given to mentally handicapped young people, who get even less than the physically handicapped. Many of them do not realize what is happening to their bodies during adolescence. A young boy may think that his wet dreams mean he is wetting the bed, and he thinks that is wrong. Menstruation can be very upsetting if a girl is not prepared physically and emotionally to cope.

A British report carried out for the Spastics Society and the National Association for Mental Health tells a story which illustrates the consequences of a lack of proper sex education: 'A young man discharged from a subnormality hospital was shortly afterwards returned as impossible to keep outside; his open masturbation was an intolerable problem. It turned out that no one had once thought to tell him that this was socially unacceptable behaviour. Now he does it in private like everyone else, and is living perfectly happily in the local community.'

So the mentally retarded need, like everyone else, the social know-how to cope with their sexuality; and this means that they need to have thorough and painstaking sex education, so that they can use sexuality in a mature and loving way.

10

The future:
aids and attitudes

A Roman Catholic priest wrote to a magazine recently about a parishioner of his, a young man of 18, who had been involved in a serious road accident and was now paralysed from the waist down. He was impotent. After re-habilitation and convalescence he was making a good recovery and was about to start light work. During his convalescence he had become friendly with a healthy girl of his own age. They fell in love. But the parents felt that the future was so bleak that the girl should be told that satisfactory marriage was out of the question. The priest, however, while agreeing that the truth should be told, felt that a marriage between them could still be wonderfully rewarding and satisfying.

'They are so involved with each other and so much in love,' he wrote, 'that a break would be shattering for them both, but especially for the boy who has already suffered so much. I feel that provided he accepts with some grace the fact that there can be no more sexual satisfaction for him and provided she accepts that she will not be able to have his children, I believe their future together could be good. Sexual fulfilment for her will be limited and for him the satisfactions of the marriage will be on another level. I believe normal sexual intercourse could be simulated by the boy wearing an artificial penis, and masturbation and oral sex can all play a part in their relationship.'

The priest has already formulated his opinions, but he felt that his ideas might be considered so revolutionary in the circles where he was going to be expressing them that he needed the support and advice of other professional counsellors. He was absolutely on the right track. As long as both young people found nothing offensive in artificial aids, then these could provide an extra dimension in their sex lives and their marriage.

Here then is straight-from-the-shoulder practical advice for the sexual problems of the handicapped, at work at the grass roots. No doubt it will shock some people to hear such an august member of the Establishment talking about dildoes and oral sex. But the story demonstrates that compassion and understanding can help people with handicaps of one kind or another to achieve a level of emotional independence and emotional satisfaction which the more able-bodied take for granted. And they have every right to it, as the priest has shown.

Not so long ago marriage between two young people such as those would have been ruled out, mainly because child-bearing was considered not only vital for marital happiness but the very *raison d'être* of marriage. To entertain the idea of artificial aids a decade ago would have been to put the whole situation into the realm of blue films and pornography. If the permissive society has achieved nothing else it has helped to free us from the old traditions of secrecy and guilt which for so long have surrounded the sex act, and enabled us to accept that different people have differing sexual needs. No one has the right to push their standards on to other people, making the assumption that their feelings and thoughts are the same.

If a 'dirty' book is the only way one man can get turned on sexually (and he is neither harming nor corrupting others), then why should he not enjoy it? And by the same token if that young couple can bring each other happiness, and if an artificial penis or a vibrator, acceptable to them both, adds scope to their relationship, then it would be wrong to deny them such substitutes on the grounds of obscenity. Dildoes and vibrators are probably only disgusting to a few of those people lucky enough to be endowed with all their organs intact.

However, these solutions may not be acceptable to everyone; and, at this stage, artificial sex aids, although they have been known and used in different societies for hundreds of years, may be the answer for only a small proportion of couples or individuals. But this is no reason to discount them as suitable only for a perverted minority.

Let us examine for a moment what we mean by

pornography and perversion, what functions they perform, and how they are relevant in the context of helping the handicapped to a more fulfilling sexual life.

Pornography may be defined as obscene literature, paintings and pictures, in fact anything intended to cause sexual excitement. A see-through black negligée, a heavy French perfume, a pair of silk stockings, are then by definition obscene! But it is undeniable that what is obscene to some is perfectly normal to others; and women's magazines, in their advice columns and, by implication, their romantic short stories, have been encouraging their women readers for donkey's years to arouse their husbands with such aids. So we push the barriers further and further back until we allow increasingly explicit films, full-frontal pin-ups in daily family newspapers, and sexually suggestive advertising for anything from cigarettes to wholemeal biscuits. None of these is actionable in terms of the legal definition of pornography, yet their purpose is sexual stimulation and titillation.

It is not until we reach the sex shops, the so-called dirty magazines and books, and the erotic underground films, that people begin to talk in terms of pornography and perversion. But where do you draw the line? And who draws it? Should we not each draw our own line? The problem is that where we each do draw that line depends on the sum of our own experiences and needs; and what society has yet to do is to accept this concept of being free to be our own censors, our own judges of what we find to be acceptable. So many people are kept busy minding other people's morals for them.

This probably sounds like a lecture from an abolitionist's pulpit. In a way it is. But more than that it is a plea for tolerance and understanding towards those who are in some way different from ourselves; because I believe that what is generally considered to be pornographic or obscene can play a vital part in the sexual lives of the severely handicapped. As long as society implies that there is some shame involved, the handicapped will either be denied access to these aids and substitutes or have their enjoyment, when they *can* get them, ruined by feelings of guilt.

Happily, an increasing number of handicapped people are finding the help they so badly need in the so-called sex shops. Men like the young man quoted earlier, who have become impotent and are unable to get an erection, are finding prostheses invaluable for regaining a feeling of manliness. These are very skilfully manufactured and incredibly life-like imitations of the penis, made in varying qualities of rubber and therefore varying in price from about £7 to £28 at the time of writing. They are frequently advertised in girlie magazines, and if anyone has any difficulty obtaining information or catalogues a family doctor or the Family Planning Association will probably be able to help. Their successful use depends on the personality and attitudes of the couple. A woman whose husband was paralysed after an industrial accident went to a marriage guidance counsellor, because she was getting very nervy and tense. She explained her own sexual frustrations, but also said how sorry she felt for her husband who previously had been a very virile individual. The counsellor suggested she might be satisfied with manual clitoral stimulation by her husband; but the woman was obviously unhappy about this. Then they got round to thinking about an artificial penis, strapped to the husband with a built-in vibrator. She was fairly reluctant at first, but agreed to try and found the method extremely satisfying. As her husband was actually involved, it also gave him a feeling of manhood and satisfaction.

Vibrators are increasingly being used in the treatment of frigidity. This is nearly always a psychological problem, and is most usually caused by emotional hang-ups, which may go back to early childhood experiences. These are sometimes so deep and involved that they totally prevent the woman from relaxing or 'letting go' enough to experience orgasm. The vibrator can overcome these physical blockages; and often the experience of orgasm is enough to begin to release the tension and anxieties, and encourage enjoyment from sexual intercourse. For the woman alone, or one in a sexual relationship with a man who is impotent, the experience of a vibrator can help restore feelings of femininity and be a source of physical and emotional release, as long as there are no feelings of guilt about using it. There are also many varieties of rubber and plastic human-shaped bodies, which are valuable for men who cannot manage to find a living partner.

The thought of these aids may seem laughable or disgusting to some, but if they are of help, they should be made freely available to those who want them.

Most libraries offer their readers a vast selection of romantic novels through which they can live their fantasy lives between washing up and getting the next meal. No one would question the propriety of this literature. This is how many women get their sexual kicks, although they probably do not realize it. Most men however need stronger meat, and they often get healthy sexual stimulation and fun from pictures of naked women. This is harmless enjoyment. It does not make men leave their wives, any more than the fortunes of Sir Galahad and the peasant girl in the women's magazines send the average woman running away from home. But even pictures of naked women pall after a while, so many men, and women as well, who do not have opportunities for interpersonal sex relationships, turn to thoroughgoing pornography for erotic stimulation. Unfortunately even the mention of the word pornography tends to make some people bridle with anger and prejudice. But there is no evidence to show that pornography corrupts; and there is plenty to show that for some people it encourages a release of built-up sexual tension, and lowers destructive antisocial feelings.

At present, pornographic literature tends to be restricted to sleazy back street bookshops. Sex aids sell at inflated prices by mail order or in the sex shops. The shops are very often located in tortuous city centres where the disabled hardly ever go unaccompanied, and mail order supplies are advertised in the kind of publication that rarely circulates in residential homes. This all makes access for the disabled somewhat difficult; but they should have the same opportunities to buy and to read as the able-bodied. Part of the answer must be to provide a wide range of newspapers and magazines in homes and clubs where the disabled meet, so that they can have the freedom of access to the basic information, and, buying or not, at least know that these things exist and are used by a wide cross-section of people for a wide variety of reasons. Pornographic material also should be available to the disabled (as it is to the able-bodied on many a bookstall), without there being any feeling of shame. This means non-judgmental attitudes on the part of those who may make it available, whether it is in residential units, clubs or other meeting places of the disabled. And there should be as wide a variety as possible, because what turns one person on does not necessarily turn on another.

The disabled need these opportunities to explore the world of pornography, because this is yet another way in which we grow as human beings: by noticing and understanding our own reactions to this kind of material we learn a little more about ourselves and about the feelings of other people. Everyone has the right to some sexual outlet if they want it, and they must be allowed to use pornography if it can help to provide it. Sexuality doesn't simply disappear with disability, so society can no longer continue to force on the weaker members standards that are unwanted and resented.

Any discussion of the future pattern of sexual life for the disabled must examine in greater depth than ever before, and with great compassion, the question of third-party sex and the use of a surrogate partner. There are cases where a disabled individual or a couple are so handicapped that it is impossible for them to perform any of the conventional sexual activities without help. I have spoken about the father who taught his son to masturbate. In some cases it will be necessary for someone able-bodied to do the masturbating for the disabled person, if that disabled person has no hands or cannot use them.

The big question-mark over this subject is who performs this function? In some residential homes there are humane staff who consider this to be part of their nursing duties, because they know their charges need the sexual release. In other cases residents perform it for other residents. For most people however it will be something they find impossible to take in their stride, especially if they are called upon to help a couple rather than an individual. Possibly it is better to allow a couple to find their own level of satisfaction, rather than accept a standard they have difficulty in achieving and for which they need the help of a third party. Many of course would be so turned off by such an intrusion that the question does not arise.

The use of surrogates entails finding a sexual partner for intercourse and sex play, who can perform without any emotional attachment but simply give the other partner the satisfaction that masturbation does not bring. Many good and caring people might be intensely shocked at the idea of providing this service for the disabled; but in spite of the

108

immense problems and obstacles that must obviously be taken into account, we must not ignore the possibility of such a service being of value.

A social worker contacted me recently to speak about a very severely disabled young man, who masturbates himself with physical but little emotional release. He feels that he desperately wants to make love to, or try to make love to, a real woman. I met the young man and spent some time with him talking about his problem. I was not convinced that he really would find the satisfaction he wanted merely by intercourse—even if he could manage. I was sure that what he really wanted was the warmth and love and caring of a heterosexual relationship. If he had been able-bodied, he would have worked this out for himself; as he was disabled, did I or anyone else have the right to prevent him testing out his own needs?

As it happens, there are as yet few girls or women available to perform this particular function—but possibly we should be exploring the possibilities of doing something about it. The difficulties and problems may seem insurmountable, but not everyone would be horrified at the possibility. Many people would be sympathetic. Two women social workers I have discussed it with reacted compassionately to the idea. One was in her 30s, very sensible, unmarried but with sexual experience; the other was in her forties and married. They both said that they had on occasion felt so sorry for some disabled young men with whom they had been in contact professionally, that they had been tempted to make love to them, to give them the sort of relief they so obviously craved and needed. In such a case the surrogate would be offering more than sex; she would be giving comfort, and a kind of loving which involves the warmth of human contact. Sex by itself may indeed not be enough; but we should remember that many thousands of men do get sexual satisfaction through relations with prostitutes. It is for each individual concerned to establish his own particular standards. The reason that so many men find masturbating unsatisfactory is that they hate the solitariness of it, the self-indulgence, the lack of communication, and the absence of someone who really cares. A heterosexual relationship, even if the involvement is made as a therapeutic gesture, or as a financial transaction, at least involves someone else.

109

Problems will doubtless arise in deciding how, and how frequently, to provide and distribute both the aids and the assistance discussed above. It will require some organization; but there is no reason why the disabled themselves should not decide how to expend their resources, and like any other adult, choose which pleasure seems to be the most desirable and rewarding. At any particular time some would choose the cinema, others might want sweets or drinks or cigarettes, others would enjoy a club, and yet others would choose sex.

Once we think about this sort of provision for men, we must also of course, in these days of increasing sexual equality, think about whether a similar type of service should be provided for women. There is no doubt that women suffer the same pains of loneliness as men; and their sexual needs, though usually not as great, certainly exist. These are difficult problems. But we must not refuse to consider them, simply because they are difficult. More discussion is needed so that those who wish to get help can do so.

A variation of the third-party/surrogate-partner solution which would probably find even less acceptance in Britain comes from Denmark. In a survey of opinions among young men with cerebral palsy, it became clear that they favoured brothels where their sexual needs could be satisfied, and which were staffed with good-hearted, understanding, well-respected ladies—a kind of Salvation Army, intelligently accepting male human beings with normal, strong emotional needs for contact and physical love. The risk here of greater emotional involvement, leading to even more suffering and longing, seemed not to concern the boys; although one stated that his sexual needs definitely increased after his first experience, without any proportionate permanent satisfaction.

The same survey refers to the widely accepted and openly advertised 'exclusive personal massage clinics' in Denmark. These too are available in parts of Britain and could be useful to the disabled in the context of sexual gratification by a third party; but the handicapped with their already under-privileged economic circumstances are never going to find the means to make use of these usually very expensive establishments, and I cannot see the Welfare State considering such a service 'within their scope' at present. A solution might be found with the organization of such services through the disabled clubs and residential units.

Clubs themselves can and do play a vital part in the lives of thousands of handicapped people. We need more, particularly where able-bodied and handicapped can meet together to share pastimes that both enjoy. These clubs provide not only ordinary socializing opportunities but also an environment in which people can test out and experiment with friendships—a chance to explore reactions, to see how others respond, and gradually to reorganize and accept the submerged parts of their own individual personalities. This social interaction is of major importance, because friendship, love and marriage cannot happen in the kind of isolation to which most disabled people are subjected.

Throughout the book, I have stressed the need for counsellors and counselling services. Unfortunately these are very thin on the ground for everyone, but even those that do exist are rarely easily available to anyone in a wheelchair, or someone who has not easy access to public transport. Few counselling services are specifically geared to the problems of the disabled, and those that are more often than not (through no fault of their own) operate in a room at the top of a flight of stairs. Doctors and social workers may be willing to help; but often they give no indication that this is so, or else they too have been given comparatively little insight during training into the problems and feelings of those who are disabled. Some of the individuals who might be able to assist become paralysed with overwhelming compassion when actually face to face with the disabled; on top of ordinary embarrassment, this puts paid to any effective communication. There are of course some organizations that provide admirable counselling services for their own disabled members, for their parents, and for the staff of residential homes. Counsellors for individual counselling and for group work are nonetheless in short supply, and there is a danger that they will be monopolized by those who have access to them and by those whose needs are already pinpointed by society.

Social workers and doctors need to be educated to help the disabled in their care. They should no longer be allowed to say either that disabled people do not have sex problems or that sex problems are not for them to solve. Their widespread

111

inability to deal with these problems—which they often blame on lack of time—is particularly unfortunate in that, if *they* refuse to help, other avenues can often be blocked as a result. Even if the doctors feel that they themselves are unable to help, they should be sensitive and perceptive enough to offer referral, if they think that it is needed.

So the disabled must press for specially trained group discussion leaders and counsellors, who can guide and support disabled people gently and impartially through the exploration of their very personal feelings and on to such topics as technical sex aids, surrogate partners, brothels, etc.—even if the discussion remains hypothetical. These discussion leaders should perhaps be established as a roving force, so that they can make themselves available throughout the country to residential homes and hostels, rehabilitation centres and clubs.

Genetic counselling centres already exist in many large cities, and there patients and their doctors can go for advice as to the chances of any particular disease or combination of diseases being inherited. There is now very often quite clear statistical evidence of the chance of any illness recurring in the children. Knowing the chances, the couple can then decide for themselves whether they wish to take the risks involved. They will most likely appreciate advice from those around them such as parents, doctors, priests or social workers; but ultimately the decision is theirs, and theirs alone.

I have already spoken about counselling, but all matters associated with sex and sexuality need to be fully aired if the disabled individual or couple is to achieve a full life. And if they, like any other members of the community, are to achieve a sense of responsibility as adults, then they must be treated as adults and allowed to make decisions on all matters which concern them, even if those around them disapprove of their decision.

They may need help and counselling to cope with problems of homosexuality and abortion, and other matters upon which those around them have strong feelings and often firm religious convictions. Denying sexual feelings and blocking sexual outlets nearly always prevents growth into a whole human being. Sex is part of humanity, and sexuality an

112

integral constituent of personality. Not everyone needs to express it physically, but whether they do or not must be their own decision, and cannot arbitrarily be decided by anyone else. It is the acceptance of these feelings both by the individual and by society that helps anyone come to terms with himself and understand his real needs in the context of human relationship.

We are all the same in this—able bodied and disabled alike. We all have our own problems, and we all have the right to find our own solutions. We all need to love and be loved; and it is misguided and unjust to pretend that one section of the community permanently likes being on the receiving end only, of care, love and consideration. It is therefore reassuring to know that the subject is beginning to be discussed and thought about. National Fund for Research into Crippling Diseases has set up a committee, 'SPOD' (Sex Problems of the Disabled), to research and advise solutions; and many other organizations such as MIND and the Family Planning Association are treating it as a matter of urgency.

Solutions cannot be found until problems are pinpointed. One of the first steps therefore is to allow the disabled to express and understand their problems.

Select Bibliography

Follow-up of cerebrally palsied married and engaged couples who attended short residential courses between April 1969 and April 1972. Spastics Society, 1972.

The Last Refuge. Townsend, P.   Routledge, 1964.

Let There Be Love. Enby, P.   Elek/Pemberton, 1975.

A Life Apart. Miller, E. J. and Gwynne, G. V.   Tavistock, 1972.

Life Together. Nordqvist, I.   Swedish Central Committee for Rehabilitation (SVCR), Stockholm, 1972.

Marriage and the Handicapped. Morgan, M.   Spastics Society, 1969.

Marriage, Sex and Arthritis. Greengross, W.   Arthritis and Rheumatism Council, 1974.

Not Made of Stone: the Sexual Problems of Handicapped People. Heslinga, K.   (Leyden and Illinois), 1974.

Personal Relationships, the Handicapped and the Community. Lancaster-Gaye, D. (ed.).   Routledge, with Cerebral Palsy Society, 1972.

Psychological and Practical Aspects of Sex and Marriage for the Paraplegic. Masham, the Baroness. Proceedings of the Royal Society of Medicine, LXVI, 1973.

A Right to Love? A Report on Public and Professional Attitudes. Shearer, A.   Spastics Society, with National Association of Mental Health, 1972.

Sex and Arthritis. Hamilton, A.   British Journal of Sexual Medicine, II.1, 1975.

Sex and the Physically Handicapped. Stewart, W. F. R.   National Fund for Research into Crippling Diseases, 1975.

Sexual Problems of Physically Disabled Adolescents. Nordqvist, I.   SVCR, Stockholm, 1973.

The Stigma. Hunt, P. (ed.).   Chapman, 1966.

Adult Adjustment of Some Deficient American Children. Charles, D. C.   American Journal of Mental Deficiency, 1957.

Biology and Mental Defect. Penrose, L. S.   Sidgwick and Jackson, 1964.

The Feebleminded Parent. Mickelson, P.   American Journal of Mental Deficiency, 1947.

114

Marriage and Mental Handicap. Mattinson, J.   Duckworth, 1970.

The Mental Defective on Licence. Middleton, T. H.   Journal of the Midland Mental Deficiency Society, 1956.

Mental Deficiency. Hilliard, L. T. and Kerman, B. H.   Churchill, 1965.

The Offspring of Mental Defectives. Proceedings of the 1st Congress of the International Association for the scientific study of mental deficiency, 1968.

Residential Care and the Adult Spastic. Loring, J.   Proceedings of the 1st Congress of the International Cerebral Palsy Society, 1971.

Sexual Rights of the Retarded. Lee, G. W.   National Society for Mentally Handicapped Children.

Sexuality, Contraception and the Mentally Retarded. Fujita, B., Wagner, N. N. and Pion, R. J.   Social Medicine, 1970.

An Analysis of Human Sexual Response. Brecher, R. and Brecher, E. (eds.).   Panther, 1969.

Homosexuality. West, D. J.   Penguin, 1969.

Intimate Behaviour. Morris, D.   Corgi, 1973.

Modern Contraception. Monton, E.   Roseneath Scientific Publications.

A New Concept in the Treatment of Sexual Dysfunction. Blakoe Ethical Products, London, 1974.

Sex Factor in Marriage. Wright, H.   Benn.

Sex in Human Loving. Berne, E.   Penguin, 1973.

Sex Manners for Men. Chartham, R.   New English Library, 1968.

Sex Manners for Women. Chartham, R.   Sphere.

Sex with Health.   WHICH Publications.

Sexual Behaviour in the Human Male. Kinsey, A.   W. B. Saunders, 1953.

Sexual Behaviour in the Human Female. Kinsey, A.   W. B. Saunders, 1953.

Sexual Techniques: An Illustrated Guide to Love. Toft, M. and Fowlie, J. Souvenir Press, 1969.

Understanding Human Sexual Inadequacy. Belliveau, F. and Richter, L. Coronet, 1971.

Further information is available from the Family Planning Association, the National Marriage Guidance Council, and the committee for Sexual Problems of the Disabled.

Index

120

LIFE
WORTH
LIVING